1 9 9 0 U P D A T E

THE
LAW OF
PUBLIC
COMMUNICATION

K E N T R. M I D D L E T O N

University of Georgia

B I L L F. C H A M B E R L I N

University of Florida

Longman
New York & London

1990 Update for The Law of Public Communication

Longman, 95 Church Street, White Plains, N.Y. 10601

Associated companies:
Longman Group Ltd., London
Longman Cheshire Pty., Melbourne
Longman Paul Pty., Auckland
Copp Clark Pitman, Toronto

Executive editor: Gordon T. R. Anderson

ISBN 0-8013-0477-6

ABCDEFGHIJ–CCP–99 98 97 96 95 94 93 92 91 90

CONTENTS

*The italicized descriptions below identify information collected for the **1990 Update** for **The Law of Public Communication**. Subheads for sections not updated are excluded. Page numbers in parentheses after bold-faced heads and subheads tell where material in the **Update** fits into **The Law of Public Communication**.*

PREFACE

This is the 1990 expanded update for *The Law of Public Communication*. It supercedes the 1989 *Update* which is now obsolete and out of print. This volume includes court cases, legislation, and administrative decisions affecting the law of public communication since the textbook went to press in the summer of 1987. During that time, the Supreme Court delivered important decisions affecting the high school press, emotional distress suits, the publication of names of rape victims, the placement of newspaper racks, picketing, the Freedom of Information Act, and corporate disclosure. In addition, lower courts issued significant opinions affecting the regulation of broadcasting and cable television. The Federal Communications Commission abolished the fairness doctrine and increased regulation of "indecent" broadcasts.

We have organized the *1990 Update* to parallel the text. The subject headings in the *1990 Update* are the same as those in the textbook. The page numbers in parentheses in the *1990 Update* refer to the place in the text in which the same subject is discussed. There are also suggestions for the appropriate placement of new sections, such as those on student expression, negligence in advertising, and the fairness doctrine.

The authors intend to issue an update each year between new editions of the text. Professors who have adopted *The Law of Public Communication* can receive a desk copy of the *1990 Update* directly from the publisher. Students buying unused copies of the text will receive the *1990 Update* with the text at no additional cost. Individual copies of the *1990 Update* may be ordered through any bookstore.

The authors wish to thank the many professors and students who already have used *The Law of Public Communication* and particularly those who have sent us comments, questions, and suggestions. We hope readers will continue to tell us what parts of the book are particularly effective and to suggest changes for future editions.

The authors would like to thank several people for helping us produce the *1990 Update*. We appreciate the research of Sherry Alexander, Linda Perry, and Sig Splichal, graduate students at the University of Florida; and Linda MacColl, a graduate assistant at the University of Georgia. Librarians who have provided special assistance include Sally Curtis Askew at the University of Georgia, and Sally Cravens and Rosalie Sanderson at the University of Florida. Christine Finnegan, former assistant to the director of the Brechner Center, and Jeanne Chamberlin edited the manuscript and proofread. Bonnie Bellew, a graduate student at the University of Florida, provided technical assistance.

Kent R. Middleton
Bill F. Chamberlin

1
PUBLIC COMMUNICATION AND THE LAW

THE COURTS

The Federal System

The U.S. Supreme Court (Add to footnote 11, p. 12)

Justice Lewis F. Powell, Jr., retired from the Court in 1988 and was replaced by Justice Anthony M. Kennedy, who had been a judge on the U.S. Court of Appeals for the Ninth Circuit. In most cases before the Supreme Court in 1989, Kennedy was part of a five-person conservative majority that included Chief Justice William H. Rehnquist and Justices Sandra Day O'Connor, Byron R. White, and Antonin Scalia.[1] However, Kennedy has joined liberal justices in key cases protecting First Amendment values. For example, Kennedy joined Justices William J. Brennan, Jr., Thurgood Marshall, Harry A. Blackmun, John Paul Stevens, and conservative Antonin Scalia in striking down a Florida law that prohibited newspapers from printing the names of rape victims. He also voted with Brennan, Marshall, Blackmun, and Scalia to hold that flag burning is protected by the First Amendment.[2]

---

[1]*See, e.g.,* Savage, "Justice Consistently Conservative; Kennedy's Record Sours Liberals' Victory on Bork," *Los Angeles Times*, June 11, 1989, at 1, and Kamen, "Divisive Issues at Center Stage as Court Term Ends," *Washington Post*, July 5, 1989, at 1.

[2]*But see,* e.g., Ward v. Rock Against Racism, 109 S. Ct. 2746 (1989) (Kennedy, J., majority opinion; a city's noise-control regulation for concerts was not a violation of the First Amendment).

2
THE FIRST AMENDMENT

In important first amendment decisions since *The Law of Public Communication* was published, the Supreme Court has upheld the right to burn the American flag and has severely limited the rights of high school journalists. The Court also has issued opinions limiting federal prisoners' access to information and regulating demonstrations, news-racks, taxes on the media, and amplification at rock concerts.

THEORY OF FREEDOM OF EXPRESSION

Right to Fulfillment

Individuals

Receiving Information (pp. 34-35) The Supreme Court ruled in 1989 that federal prisoners may be denied access to publications under "reasonable" regulations that protect prison security.   In *Thornburgh v. Abbott*, a 6-3 majority upheld federal regulations denying prisoners a publication the warden considers "detrimental to the security, good order, or discipline of the institution or if it might facilitate criminal activity." In an opinion written by Justice Blackmun, the majority found the federal regulations constitutional because they "reasonably related to legitimate penological interests." The Court approved the broad discretion accorded wardens to withhold publications that could exacerbate tensions and lead to disorder.[1]

---

[1] 57 U.S.L.W. 4517 (May 15, 1989).

The Court said the federal regulations that ensure prison security operate in a constitutionally neutral fashion because they do not permit exclusion of a publication "solely because its content is religious, philosophical, political, social or sexual, or because its content is unpopular or repugnant."

While prisoners may be denied information, other Americans may have access to more information than before. Recent legislation may increase access to foreign speakers. In the Foreign Relations Authorization Act, Congress prohibited the State Department from denying visas because of foreigners' political beliefs or associations or because of what they might say in the United States.[2] While the legislation creates no constitutional right of access for Americans to foreign speakers, the legislation may permit Americans greater contact with Communists and other foreign speakers the government opposes. However, under the act, the State Department retains power to deny visas to foreigners with criminal records and to foreigners who might be expected to engage in terrorism in the United States.

The legislative restriction on the denial of visas followed a federal appeals court. decision preventing the State Department from denying visas to foreign speakers with alleged Communist ties. The U.S. Court of Appeals for the D. C. Circuit ruled the State Department could bar entry to Communists only if they pose a threat to the public safety or to the security of the country.[3] The case arose when the State Department denied visas to Tomas Borge, Nicaraguan interior minister; Nino Pasti, a former Italian general and a member of a peace group; and two members of a Cuban women's group.

The Supreme Court upheld the appeals court decision by a 3-3 vote. The evenly-split vote affirming the D.C. Circuit means that the *Abourezk* holding is binding only in the District of Columbia. Although visas are typically issued or denied by American consular officials stationed at embassies abroad,[4] appeals of visa denials are usually filed in federal court in Washington. The unusual 3-3 vote in the Supreme Court occurred because Justice Kennedy was not yet appointed to fill the seat vacated when Justice Powell retired, and two other justices did not participate.

High School Students (New section to be inserted before Associations, p. 35) In 1969, the Supreme Court said freedom of expression does not stop at the school house door.[5] But in January 1988, the Supreme Court ruled *in Hazelwood School District v. Kuhlmeier* (p. 371) that high school principals may censor nearly all student expression sponsored by, or associated with, the school.[6]

---

[2]"News Media Alert," *News Media & Law* 14 (Spring 1988).

[3]Abourezk v. Reagan, 785 F.2d 1043 (D.C. Cir. 1983), *aff'd by split vote*, 108 S. Ct. 252 (1987).

[4]Shapiro, "Ideological Exclusions: Closing the Border to Political Dissidents," 100 *Harv. L. Rev.* 930, 932 (1987).

[5]Tinker v. Des Moines Independent School District, 393 U.S. 503, 506 (1969). See pp. 34 and 371 of text.

[6]108 S. Ct. 562 (1988).

In May 1983, Robert Reynolds, principal of Hazelwood East High School in St. Louis County, Missouri, deleted two pages of the last issue of the school newspaper, *Spectrum*, because he objected to two articles, one about teen pregnancies, the other about divorce. Reynolds said he feared the article about three pregnant Hazelwood students would invade the girls' privacy. Even though the students in the story were given fictitious names, Reynolds said the girls might be identified from the text. Reynolds said he also thought references in the pregnancy story to sexual activity and birth control were inappropriate for younger students at the school.

Reynolds said he deleted the story about divorce because he thought parents referred to in the story should have a chance to respond. One named student complained in the story that her father "was always out of town on business or out late playing cards with the guys."

Students from the Journalism II class that produced the paper argued that the principal of Hazelwood East violated their First Amendment rights by censoring expression that posed no threat of disrupting the school. The students relied on the Supreme Court's 1969 ruling in *Tinker v. Des Moines Independent School District*.[7] The Supreme Court held in *Tinker* that high school students had a First Amendment right to wear black arm bands to protest the war in Vietnam. In *Tinker*, the Court said that high school students have a constitutional right to express themselves unless their expression "materially disrupts classwork or involves substantial disorder or invasion of the rights of others."

In *Hazelwood*, the Court refused to apply the "disruption" standard from *Tinker*, ruling instead that high school officials may censor school-sponsored expression whenever the regulation is "reasonably related to legitimate pedagogical concerns." The Court, in a decision written by Justice White, said the disruption standard is appropriate in cases of students' "personal expression," such as the black arm bands in *Tinker*, but is not required in cases of "school-sponsored expressive activities," such as the newspaper in *Hazelwood*. Where student expression is part of the curriculum, as the Hazelwood newspaper was ruled to be, schools may regulate it in any reasonable way, White said.

Hazelwood students had argued that *Spectrum* was not part of the curriculum, but was a "public forum," like a sidewalk or public park (p. 68). As a public forum, the newspaper was dedicated to robust discussion of public issues, the students said. To support their claim that the Hazelwood School District had made *Spectrum* a public forum, students pointed out that the school had adopted policies guaranteeing publication of "diverse viewpoints." Students also noted that *Spectrum* was published every three weeks during the school year and that more than 4,500 copies of the newspaper were distributed during the year to students, school personnel, and members of the community. The paper was not just a classroom exercise, the students said.

However, Justice White said *Spectrum* was a "supervised learning experience for journalism students." White called *Spectrum* a "laboratory" paper because it was published in Journalism II, a class that was part of the school curriculum. *Spectrum*,

---

[7]393 U.S. 503.

unlike a street corner or public park, had not been continuously used "for purposes of assembly, communicating thought between citizens, and discussing public questions," White said. Nor, he continued, had school officials opened the school paper, as public sidewalks have been, "for indiscriminate use by the general public." To distinguish *Spectrum* from a public forum, Justice White pointed out that the newspaper advisor in Journalism II selected the editor, edited stories, and sought approval from the principal for each issue before publication.

The majority in *Hazelwood* did not limit official control to student newspapers produced in a journalism class. The Court said school officials retain authority over any expressive activities associated with the school, including school-sponsored publications, theatrical productions, and other expressive activities that appear to bear the school's imprimatur. To Justice White, all expression associated with a high school "may fairly be characterized as part of the school curriculum," even if it does not occur in a traditional classroom. All student expression may be regulated if it is "supervised by faculty members and designed to impart particular knowledge or skills to student participants and audiences."[8]

The Court also said that "reasonable" regulations on student expression are not limited to the concerns about privacy and fairness at issue in the Hazelwood East newspaper. High school officials, White said, may control student expression

> to assure that participants learn whatever lessons the activity is designed to teach, that readers or listeners are not exposed to material that may be inappropriate for their level of maturity, and that the views of the individual speaker are not erroneously attributed to the school. Hence, a school may in its capacity as publisher of a school newspaper or producer of a school play "disassociate itself," not only from speech that would "substantially interfere with [its] work . . . or impinge upon the rights of other students," but also from speech that is, for example, ungrammatical, poorly written, inadequately researched, biased or prejudiced, vulgar or profane, or unsuitable for immature audiences.[9]

For the majority in *Kuhlmeier*, the school's responsibility is to help awaken children to "cultural values," not to encourage maximum free expression under the First Amendment. Schools, the Court said quoting *Bethel School District v. Fraser* (pp. 370-371), are not required to sponsor student speech that is inconsistent with "the shared values of a civilized social order."

Given the broad powers of school administrators to control student expression in *Kuhlmeier*, the Court had no difficulty deciding that the principal of Hazelwood East

---

[8] 108 S. Ct. at 570.

[9] *Id.*

acted reasonably when he deleted two pages of *Spectrum*. Justice White said it was reasonable for the principal to conclude that the anonymity of the students quoted in the article about pregnancy was not sufficiently protected because of identifying information in the article and the small number of pregnant students at the school. Furthermore, White said it was reasonable for Reynolds to be concerned that the article was not sufficiently sensitive to the privacy of the students' boyfriends and parents who were discussed in the piece.

The Court said it was also reasonable for the principal to conclude that frank talk in the article about the girls' sexual history and failure to use birth control was inappropriate in a school-sponsored publication distributed to 14-year-old students and perhaps taken home to be read by younger brothers and sisters. In addition, the Court said it was reasonable for the principal to conclude that journalistic fairness required that the father portrayed as inattentive in the article about divorce be given an opportunity to reply.

Justice Brennan, in a very sharp dissent joined by Justices Marshall and Blackmun, argued that the wide powers of censorship granted to administrators by the majority threatened to create "enclaves of totalitarianism" in the public schools. Brennan said the First Amendment does not permit a school to bar student communication simply because it may be at odds with a school's pedagogical message.

Official censorship should not be used, Brennan said, to shield the audience or dissociate the sponsor from expression. Such censorship, he said, cannot serve the curricular purposes of a student newspaper "unless one believes that the purpose of the school newspaper is to teach students that the press ought never . . . upset its sponsors." Brennan said the majority's decision teaches students that principles of free speech are "mere platitudes." Students who enrolled in Journalism II at Hazelwood East High School expected a civics lesson, Brennan said with heavy irony, "but not the one the Court teaches them today."

The Supreme Court's decision in *Hazelwood* does not bar distribution on high school and university campuses of "underground" or "alternative" publications that are not sponsored by the school. Such expression is, like the arm bands in *Tinker*, personal to the student. However, off-campus publications may be barred on high school campuses, the U.S. Court of Appeals for the Eighth Circuit has ruled, if they would disrupt teaching, if they are libelous or obscene to minors, if they are "pervasively indecent or vulgar," or if they advertise products illegal to minors.[10]

*College Students (New section to be inserted before **Associations** on p. 35)* The *Kuhlmeier* decision deals with expression in public high schools, not public colleges and universities. *Kuhlmeier* does not say whether officials at state colleges and universities have the same powers as high school principals to censor school-sponsored expression. But in a case involving an off-campus publication, the Supreme Court ruled several years ago that university officials do not have the authority to ban offensive student expression.

---

[10]Bystrom v. Fridley High School, 822 F.2d 747, 14 Med. L. Rptr. 1517 (1987).

In a 1973 decision, *Papish v. Board of Curators*,[11] the Supreme Court held that the University of Missouri could not put Barbara Papish, a graduate student in journalism, on probation for distributing the *Free Press Underground*, an off-campus paper. One issue of the paper contained a political cartoon depicting a club-wielding policeman raping the Statue of Liberty. Inside the paper was an article headlined, "Motherfucker Acquitted." The article concerned the acquittal of a New York youth for assault and battery. The university said the publication was "indecent conduct or speech," and its distribution violated the by-laws of the University's Board of Curators.

The University of Missouri Board of Curators won in the U.S. Court of Appeals for the Eighth Circuit, but the decision was overturned by the U.S. Supreme Court. In its 6-3 decision, the Supreme Court said that the "mere dissemination of ideas--no matter how offensive to good taste--on a state university campus may not be shut off in the name alone of 'conventions of decency.'" Contrary to the Court's high school decision in *Kuhlmeier*, the Court in *Papish* also said that college students cannot be held to a higher standard of expressive conduct on a state university campus than off campus. The First Amendment, the Court said in *Papish*, "leaves no room for the creation of a dual standard in the academic community with respect to the content of speech."

Government Employees (New section to be inserted before Associations on p. 35) In June 1987, a divided Supreme Court established a broad constitutional right for low-level government employees to engage in hostile conversations at work. In *Rankin v. McPherson*, the Court ruled 5-4 that Ardith McPherson could not be fired from her clerical job in the Harris County, Texas, constable's office for saying she hoped President Reagan would be assassinated.[12]

In 1981, shortly after hearing of an attempt on President Reagan's life, McPherson said to a co-worker, "If they go for him again, I hope they get him." McPherson said she "didn't mean anything" by the statement, which was part of a conversation about how the Reagan administration had cut Medicaid benefits and food stamps. A fellow employee, who overheard the remark, reported it to a superior who fired McPherson.

The Supreme Court balanced a government employer's interest in promoting office efficiency against an employee's right as a citizen to comment upon matters of public concern. The majority, in an opinion written by Justice Marshall, said that McPherson's remark dealt with a matter of public concern because it was made during a conversation about the president's policies just after an attempt on his life. Both the administration's policies and an assassination attempt are matters of public concern.

The Court said a threat to kill the president would not be protected by the First Amendment. However, McPherson's comment was ruled to be a caustic and unpleasantly sharp verbal attack on a public official that was within the robust debate protected by the First Amendment. Furthermore, the majority found no evidence that McPherson's comment interfered with the efficient functioning of the constable's office.

---

[11]410 U.S. 667.

[12]107 S. Ct. 2891.

Justice Scalia, joined by Chief Justice Rehnquist and Justices White and O'Connor, dissented. The dissenters argued that McPherson's comments were similar to an assassination threat or "fighting words," expression that is beyond First Amendment protection. Scalia said he did not understand how the majority could consider a statement approving a violent crime to be protected speech about a matter of public concern.

Associations (pp. 35-36)

The Supreme Court ruled in 1989 that a California election code prohibiting political endorsements by the governing bodies of political parties was unconstitutional. In *March Fong EU v. San Francisco County Democratic Central Committee*, the Court ruled that the state law, which also regulated election to leadership positions in state and county central committees and state party conventions, violated rights of free speech and association.[13]

The law was enacted to promote party stability. It was feared that parties splintered over endorsements might bring chaos to democratic processes. But the Supreme Court said in an 8-0 decision that preventing party factionalism is not a sufficient interest to justify infringements on constitutionally protected political speech and the right of association. A state law cannot bar the leaders of political parties from making endorsements that could not be barred if made by newspapers and other organizations, the Court said. Furthermore, the Court said, voters benefit from party leaders' evaluation of a candidate's fitness for office. Chief Justice Rehnquist did not participate in the case.

Solicitation (p. 36) An Illinois appellate court ruled that newspapers soliciting subscriptions door-to-door are exempt from a suburban ordinance requiring commercial solicitors to have a permit. The Court ruled that no permit may be required for a newspaper subscription solicitation because the subscription campaign is like a non-commercial solicitation for political, charitable, or religious purposes, all of which are protected by the First Amendment.[14]

RESTRICTING EXPRESSION

Bias Against Content Regulations

Hierarchy of Protected Expression

Political and Cultural Expression (pp. 51-52) In one of the most controversial U.S. Supreme Court cases in recent years, the Court reversed the conviction of Gregory Lee Johnson for burning an American flag in violation of a Texas statute. The Court ruled

---

[13]57 U.S.L.W. 4251 (Feb. 22, 1989).

[14]Chicago Tribune v. Downers Grove, 508 N.E.2d 439, 14 Med. L. Rptr. 1273 (Ill. App. 1987).

5-4 that the Texas law, which prohibited intentional desecration of the flag when such desecration "seriously offend[s]" others, unconstitutionally punished Johnson for expression of protected political opinion.[15]

Johnson burned the flag during the 1984 Republican National Convention in Dallas to protest policies of the Reagan administration. Johnson set the flag on fire after dousing it with kerosene in front of City Hall. While the flag burned, protestors chanted, "America, the red, white, and blue, we spit on you." Several witnesses testified that they had been seriously offended, but no one was injured or threatened with injury.

In *Texas v. Johnson*, the Court rejected Texas' argument that the statute was a neutral law protecting public property. Texas argued that the flag is a symbol of national unity, which the state may protect from desecration, much as the federal government protects the Lincoln Memorial and other public property from graffiti artists. No one may paint the Lincoln Memorial, regardless of the message.

The Court, however, said the Texas statute was not a neutral regulation. Unlike a content-neutral ban on spray painting, the Texas statute only punished flag burners when the public was offended. The Texas statute would not be invoked if a patriot respectfully burned a damaged flag. The Texas statute, therefore, punished Johnson for what he expressed, not merely how he expressed it. Furthermore, the Court said, what Johnson expressed in his symbolic act was constitutionally protected political opinion.

The majority, in an opinion by Justice Brennan, rejected Texas' argument that Johnson's conviction was justified because the flag burning threatened a riot. The Court noted there was no evidence of a riot, and Johnson was not charged with incitement or breach of the peace.

The Court also rejected Texas' argument that punishment was necessary to protect the flag as a symbol of national unity. The United States has a long history of protecting expression that is critical, defiant, and contemptuous of the flag and other national symbols, Justice Brennan wrote for the majority. Just as the First Amendment prohibits compelled flag salutes (p. 36), the First Amendment also bars punishment for offensive expressions of disrespect, Brennan said.

Respect for the flag and national unity should be fostered, Brennan said, through persuasion and example, not through punishment of flag burners. Brennan suggested that the Court's protection of a flag burner might even increase respect for the flag as a symbol of freedom.

In a dissenting opinion, Chief Justice Rehnquist said he considered the public burning of the American flag to be "no essential part of any exposition of ideas." To the Chief Justice, burning a flag is like an "inarticulate grunt or roar" that might easily be regulated by the government because it is not speech. Rehnquist, who was joined in dissent by Justices White and O'Connor, also said that Johnson's flag burning had a tendency to incite a breach of the peace.

Shortly after the Court's decision was handed down, President Bush asked for a constitutional amendment to prohibit flag burning.

---

[15]*Texas v. Johnson*, 57 U.S.L.W. 4770 (1989).

Prior Restraints

Injunctions (pp. 61-64) The Supreme Court refused to review a federal appeals court decision permitting a newspaper to ignore a "transparently invalid" restraining order (*In re Providence Journal*, p. 64). The Supreme Court dismissed a writ of *certiorari* it had earlier granted because the special prosecutor who filed the petition was not authorized to represent the government in the case. The *Providence Journal* case is discussed further in Chapter 9 of the *Update*.

Discriminatory Taxation (pp. 66-67) In 1989, the Supreme Court in a 6-3 ruling struck down a Texas law that exempted religious publications from a sales tax. In *Texas Monthly, Inc. v. Bullock*, the majority sided with the *Texas Monthly*, a general interest magazine, that argued the tax was unconstitutionally discriminatory. Five of the six justices in the majority said the Texas law violated the First Amendment provisions separating church and state.[16] Justice White, who concurred in the ruling, argued that the case was like *Arkansas Writers' Project, Inc. v. Ragland* (p. 67), in which the Court ruled a discriminatory tax is an unconstitutional restriction on freedom of expression.

Courts in California[17] and Colorado[18] upheld general business taxes that did not discriminate against publications, but several attempts to extend general taxes to advertising have failed. Bills to tax advertising were voted down in 1989 in Massachusetts and Colorado. Earlier, the Florida legislature repealed the state's five percent sales tax on services, including advertising. The tax, which had been in effect for five months, was opposed from the beginning by the Association of National Advertisers. Advertisers filed suits charging the tax violated the First Amendment, but the Florida Supreme Court ruled otherwise in an advisory opinion. The state lost millions of dollars when businesses refused to advertise and groups cancelled conventions in Florida.

Noncontent Regulations: Time, Place, and Manner (pp. 67-71)

During the last two years, the Supreme Court issued several decisions regulating demonstrations, the placement of newsracks, the loudness of rock concerts, and other expressive conduct.

In 1988, a divided Court struck down a District of Columbia code provision barring signs near foreign embassies. In *Boos v. Barry*, a five-person majority declared unconstitutional a provision prohibiting signs within 500 feet of an embassy if the signs were designed to bring a foreign government "into public odium."[19]

---

[16]108 S. Ct. 2842.

[17]Times-Mirror Co. v. City of Los Angeles, 192 Cal. App. 3d 170, 237 Cal. Rptr. 346, 14 Med. L. Rptr. 1289, *appeal dismissed*, 198 S. Ct. 743 (1988). *But see*, Redwood Empire Publishing Co. v. California State Board of Equalization, 16 Med. L. Rptr. 1257 (Cal. App. 1989).

[18]Catholic Archdiocese of Denver v. Denver, 741 P.2d 333, 14 Med. L. Rptr. 1964 (Colo. 1987).

[19]108 S. Ct. 1005 (1988).

Michael Boos challenged the law when he was prevented from displaying a sign stating "RELEASE SAKHAROV" in front of the Soviet Embassy. Another plaintiff in the case wanted to display a sign reading "STOP THE KILLING" in front of the Nicaraguan Embassy.

In a three-person plurality opinion written by Justice O'Connor, the Court said the provision barring the signs was an unconstitutional content-based restriction because it made the ability of demonstrators to display political signs in a public forum depend "entirely upon whether their picket signs are critical of the foreign government." Signs supporting a foreign government were permitted under the law, but unfavorable signs were not.

The code was defended as necessary to preserve the dignity of foreign diplomatic personnel as required by international law. But the Supreme Court said the "dignity" of diplomats was not a sufficiently compelling government interest to justify barring free expression. The plurality also found a "dignity" standard too subjective to apply in cases involving free speech. The Court also said the statute barring signs was not sufficiently narrow.

The Court upheld the constitutionality of another provision in the Washington, D.C., code limiting groups of people near foreign embassies. The code, as interpreted by the courts, permits officials to disperse crowds near an embassy only if the officials "reasonably believe that a threat to the security or peace of the embassy is present."

In another time, place, and manner decision, the Court upheld an ordinance prohibiting picketing in front of a residence. In *Frisby v. Schultz*, the Court upheld a Brookfield, Wisconsin, ban on picketing "before or about the residence or dwelling" of anyone in Brookfield, a suburb of Milwaukee.[20] The ordinance was adopted in 1985 to stop opponents of abortion from picketing in front of the home of Dr. Benjamin Victoria, a physician who performed abortions. The pickets, sometimes numbering more than 40, were peaceful, but they shouted slogans, sometimes trespassed, and told neighborhood children the doctor was a "baby killer."

Writing for a six-justice majority, Justice O'Connor said the ordinance was constitutional because it prohibited only "focused picketing taking place solely in front of a particular residence." The majority said the city could constitutionally ban picketing directed to a particular residence because such expression could invade the privacy of a "captive audience" within the home by forcing occupants to hear speech. "One important aspect of residential privacy," O'Connor said, "is protection of the unwilling listener."

Applying the Court's usual analysis in cases of time, place, and manner restrictions on speech in public forums, the Court said the ordinance is content neutral because it does not halt a specific message. The ordinance is also sufficiently narrow, as Justice O'Connor interpreted it, because it only bars picketing in front of a particular residence. The Court also noted that picketers are free to march and hand out leaflets elsewhere in the community. "General marching through residential neighborhoods, or even walking a route in front of an entire block of houses, is not prohibited by the ordinance," she said.

---

[20]*S. Ct. Bull.* B3577 (June 27, 1988).

In another time, place, and manner decision, the Supreme Court ruled that an ordinance barring newsracks in residential areas is unconstitutional. In *City of Lakewood v. Plain Dealer Publishing Co.,*[21] the Court struck down an Ohio ordinance requiring a permit from the mayor before a newspaper publisher could place newsracks on public sidewalks. In *Lakewood*, the Court ruled the city ordinance was unconstitutional on its face because it gave too much discretion to a public official to determine whether expression may be distributed. Even though the ordinance required the mayor to state reasons for denying a permit, the Court ruled 4-3 that the ordinance was unconstitutional because it vested "unbridled discretion" in a government official.

Like the ordinances struck down in the pamphleteering cases of the 1930s and 1940s (p. 68), the Lakewood ordinance gave a public official such discretion over the distribution of protected content that the ordinance created an unconstitutional form of licensing. A licensing statute "placing unbridled discretion in the hands of a government official or agency," Justice Brennan wrote for the Court, "constitutes a prior restraint and may result in censorship." The licensor's unfettered discretion intimidates parties into censoring their own speech, even if the discretion is never abused, Brennan said.

The Court saw opportunities for the Lakewood mayor to abuse his discretion because the ordinance required newspaper companies to return each year to renew their permits to place newsracks on city sidewalks. A newspaper that depends on the mayor's approval each year may feel compelled to support the mayor's policies, the Court said.

Justice White, dissenting with Justices Stevens and O'Connor, argued that the ordinance should not be struck down as invalid on its face because newspapers have no First Amendment right to place newsracks on sidewalks in the first place. The government cannot bar distribution of a newspaper, the dissenters said, but the government does not have to provide public sidewalks for newsracks if it does not want to. There are many alternatives to newsracks by which publishers may distribute their papers, the dissenters said.

In a case involving the loudness of rock music, the Supreme Court upheld regulations requiring that New York City provide and operate the sound system for groups performing in Central Park. The city adopted the regulations after area residents complained of too much noise at some events and audiences complained of too little amplification at others. Rock Against Racism, an anti-racist rock group, charged the regulations violated their right of expression. In a 6-3 decision, the Court ruled that the regulations were content neutral and narrowly tailored to provide adequate amplification without disturbing surrounding neighborhoods.[22]

---

[21]108 S. Ct. 2138 (1988).

[22]Ward v. Rock Against Racism, 109 S. Ct. 2746 (1989).

3
LIBEL

Two insurance companies and a professional journalism organization reported fewer libel suits have been filed against media companies recently. However, the threat of large damage awards still looms. In June 1988, the U.S. Supreme Court ruled, in a non-libel case, that punitive damages assessed against defendants in civil suits are constitutional. Appellate courts affirmed multi-million dollar damage claims in at least two cases. NBC has appealed $5 million in damages awarded to Wayne Newton in his libel suit against the network.

Northwestern University's Washington Annenberg Program has proposed a model libel reform statute that would significantly reduce the risk of large monetary awards in libel suits.

In 1989, the U.S. Supreme Court said an Ohio newspaper published a story about a municipal election with *New York Times* actual malice.

In one sense, libel appears to be less of a problem for the media than it was in the early 1980's. The Society of Professional Journalists (SPJ) and two libel insurance companies have reported a marked decline in the number of libel suits being filed. SPJ reported that 31 major newspapers and broadcast organizations reported fewer suits in 1988 than in 1987. Media/Professional Insurance Inc. said that the number of libel suits filed against the media decreased by a third since the fall of 1985. Mutual Insurance Co. said the average number of libel suits filed between 1985 and 1987 dropped 17 per cent from the average number filed between 1981 and 1985.[1]

---

[1]Society of Professional Journalists, *Media Litigation '88* (Nov. 4, 1988); Wong, "In Wake of Westmoreland, Sharon Cases, Libel Suits against the Media Decline," *Wall Street Journal*, Oct. 17, 1988, at B8.

The SPJ report credits part of the decrease in libel cases to the unsuccessful suits of Gen. William C. Westmoreland, Gen. Ariel Sharon of Israel, and former Mobil Oil President William Tavoulareas. None of the three men received any damages from the news media after long and expensive libel trials. The three cases, SPJ said, demonstrated the difficulty that public officials and public figures have when trying to prove *New York Times* actual malice (p.120). The study said the malice requirement has produced a "chilling effect on potential libel plaintiffs." In addition, the SPJ report indicated, lawyers are reluctant to take expensive, risky cases on the condition they get paid only if they win the case. Lawyers also claim the number of libel suits has dropped because media organizations are doing a better job of handling complaints and providing more editorial supervision of investigative reporting.

However, an attorney for the *New York Times*, George Freeman, said the decline in libel litigation has not reached the smaller newspapers. Freeman said that people in small towns are more likely than urban residents to believe that a critical story damages them. Freeman said people in small towns often think a libel suit is the only way they can fight back. The *Times* owns several small daily newspapers.[2]

THE PLAINTIFF'S BURDEN OF PROOF

Fault

New York Times *Actual Malice (pp. 120-126)*

In June 1989, the U.S. Supreme Court unanimously affirmed lower court decisions holding that a small Ohio newspaper published a story about an election for municipal judge with *New York Times* actual malice.

In *Harte-Hanks Communications v. Connaughton*, the Court upheld a $200,000 libel award for the losing judicial candidate, Daniel Connaughton, in his suit against the *Hamilton Journal News*.[3] Connaughton sued the paper for reporting the accusation of local resident Alice Thompson that Connaughton had used "dirty tricks" in his effort to oust the incumbent municipal judge, James Dolan. In a story published during the week before the election, Thompson said that Connaughton offered her and her sister jobs for themselves, jobs for their parents, and a vacation in Florida in return for information they provided for a criminal investigation of a key Dolan employee.

The Supreme Court agreed with the U.S. Court of Appeals for the Sixth Circuit that the evidence "unmistakably" supported a jury finding that the *Journal News* had exercised *New York Times* actual malice. The Supreme Court, noting the parallels between *Connaughton* and *Curtis Publishing Co. v. Butts* (pp. 121-123), said the *Journal News* intentionally avoided the truth in its preparation of the Connaughton story. The

---

[2]"Libel Suits Wane, Press Study Finds," *New York Times*, Dec. 3, 1988, at 12.

[3]109 S. Ct. 2678, 16 Med. L. Rptr. 1881 (1989).

Court said that a failure to adequately investigate a news story does not by itself constitute *New York Times* actual malice, but the *Journal News* made a "deliberate decision not to acquire knowledge . . . that might confirm the probable falsity of Thompson's charges."

The Supreme Court said the *Journal News* staff should have suspected Thompson's allegations were false because of her dislike for Connaughton and indications that she was mentally unstable. Also, Thompson's story was contradicted by six people the paper had interviewed. In addition, the paper's staff did not interview Thompson's sister, the person in the best position to corroborate or contradict her story. Neither did the staff did listen to tapes of Connaughton's principal interview with Thompson's sister, tapes that might have verified Thompson's claims. Further, the Court said, a *Journal News* editorial published before the paper had completed interviewing for the story seemed to predict the outcome of the paper's investigation. Finally, the Court said, the *Connaughton* jury apparently did not believe the newspaper staff's explanations for the incomplete investigation. For example, the Court said, the jury must have rejected staff member contentions that they believed Thompson's allegations to be substantially true.

The Supreme Court said that evidence the *Journal News* printed the Connaughton story to further an editorial policy or boost circulation could be a factor in a decision that the newspaper acted with actual malice. The Sixth Circuit emphasized in its decision that the *Journal News* had published the Connaughton story because it opposed Connaughton's candidacy and wanted a competitive advantage over a "bitter rival," the *Cincinnati Enquirer*. The Supreme Court said that a newspaper's collective state of mind, including commercial and political motives, could be one issue--but not the only one--in deciding whether a paper acted with actual malice.

The Supreme Court also used *Connaughton* to re-emphasize that public officials must prove *New York Times* actual malice in order to win libel cases. In addition, the Court reasserted that appellate courts must independently examine the basis of jury verdicts in libel cases to ensure that plaintiffs provide clear and convincing evidence that a story was published with knowing falsehood or reckless disregard for the truth.

Damages (pp. 131-134)

In 1989, the U.S. Supreme Court twice supported the ability of plaintiffs in civil suits, including libel, to sue for punitive damages. In a case unrelated to libel law, the Court said that million-dollar punitive damage awards in civil cases are constitutional. The court upheld a jury decision ordering a Vermont waste-collection company to pay $6 million in punitive damages to a competitor it had tried to force out of business. The Supreme Court said the Eighth Amendment of the Constitution prohibiting excessive fines did not apply to cases involving two private parties. Rather, the Court said, the Eighth Amendment protects individuals from government abuse.[4]

---

[4]Browning-Ferris Industries of Vermont Inc. v. Kelco Disposal Inc., 109 S. Ct. 2909 (1989).

The Court also denied review of a newspaper's appeal of a $2.2 million libel judgment, all but $200,000 for punitive damages. The Court rejected a petition of *certiorari* by the *Pittsburgh Post-Gazette*, which had argued that punitive damage awards violated the First and Fourteenth Amendments as well as the Eighth.[5] Many media lawyers had hoped the Court would rule in at least one of the two cases that large punitive damage awards are unconstitutional.

In 1988, the Court refused to review a lower court's decision awarding $3.5 million to the Brown & Williamson Tobacco Corporation for a libelous television commentary. The tobacco company had sued CBS after commentator Walter Jacobson of WBBM-TV accused the company of trying to sell Viceroy cigarettes to children (pp. 83-84). Jacobson said Viceroy's strategy was to convince young people that smoking cigarettes was an "illicit pleasure" such as drinking alcoholic beverages, smoking pot, and engaging in sexual activities. Brown & Williamson provided evidence in a federal district court that the company had rejected the "illicit pleasure" strategy and fired the ad agency that proposed it.

A jury found Jacobson's accusation to be false and awarded Brown & Williamson $3 million in compensatory damages and $2.5 million in punitive damages, but the judge reduced compensatory damages to $1. The judge said that Brown & Williamson had not proven any actual damages such as lost sales.[6] On appeal, the U.S. Court of Appeals for the Seventh Circuit reinstated $1 million in compensatory damages and upheld the award of $2.5 million in punitive damages.[7]

The award to Brown & Williamson was the first million-dollar libel judgment to be approved by an appellate court, according to the Libel Defense Resource Center (LDRC). The $2.2 million judgment against the *Pittsburgh Post-Gazette* reported above is a second.

An appeal is pending on an even larger multi-million dollar verdict. NBC has announced it will appeal the $5.3 million in libel damages awarded to Las Vegas entertainer Wayne Newton. In early 1989, Newton said he would accept the $5.3 million judgment rather than require a new libel trial. Newton had first said he wanted a new trial to reconsider the size of the award after trial judge Myron Crocker reduced the jury award of $19.3 million. However, Newton changed his mind when Crocker said a new trial would not only reconsider the size of the award, but also whether NBC ought to be liable at all.[8]

---

[5]*See* Disalle v. P.B. Publishing Co., 557 A.2d 724, 15 Med. L. Rptr. 1873 (Pa. 1988), *cert. denied*, 109 S.Ct. 3216 (1989).

[6]Brown & Williamson Tobacco Corp. v. Jacobson, 644 F. Supp. 1240, 13 Med. L. Rptr. 1263 (1986).

[7]Brown & Williamson Tobacco Corp. v. Jacobson, 827 F.2d 1119, 14 Med. L. Rptr. 1497 (1987), *cert. denied*, 108 S. Ct. 1302 (1988).

[8]"News Notes: Newton Retrial to Consider Both Liability and Damages," 15 Med. L. Rptr., Jan. 17, 1989, and "News Notes: Newton Accepts Reduced Damages Award," 15 Med. L. Rptr., Jan. 31, 1989.

Newton sued NBC for giving viewers the impression that he had asked an organized crime figure, Guido Penosi, to help him raise money to buy the Aladdin Hotel and Casino. NBC had implied that Penosi obtained a hidden interest in the casino, a violation of Nevada law. Crocker criticized the size of the jury's award to Newton for being excessive. He said that Newton's "outstanding reputation" had not been damaged by NBC and that Newton had not proven that the broadcasts had caused serious financial loss.[9]

In another recent multi-million dollar libel case, a jury in August 1989 awarded the GTE Corporation $100 million in damages in its suit against the Home Shopping Network. The Home Shopping Network, in a news release, had accused GTE of providing inadequate telephone equipment that cost the network millions of missed calls and $500 million in profits.[10] If the verdict of the Clearwater, Florida, jury is sustained on appeal, it will be the largest libel damage award in history.

However, large jury awards are frequently reduced on appeal. The Libel Defense Resource Center said in 1988 that although a large number of million-dollar trial verdicts were reported in 1985 and 1986, the average size of awards affirmed on appeal during that time was $145,000. The LDRC reported that in 11 of the 61 cases studied, damage awards announced by trial courts were greater than $1 million. Yet the LDRC said that during 1985 and 1986 no damage award of more than $50,000 was affirmed by an appellate court. The LDRC also said media libel defendants lost 72 percent of the cases that went to trial.[11] Seventy six percent of all libel suits were dismissed before a trial had begun.

The problem of large damage awards was one of the concerns of the Libel Reform Project, sponsored by an affiliate of Northwestern University. In 1988, Northwestern's Washington Annenberg Program proposed several alternatives to current libel law. An Annenberg study group, representing both the media and media critics, prepared a model statute that would focus libel disputes on establishing the truth or falsity of a story and would eliminate most large damage awards.

The Annenberg Program, an organization that sponsors research and seminars on media-related public policies, launched the project because of widespread dissatisfaction with libel laws. Lawyers representing both the media and libel plaintiffs claim that libel disputes take too much time and money. In addition, on the one hand, the threat of libel suits has forced media executives to strongly consider cutting back on aggressive journalism. On the other hand, libel plaintiffs are seldom satisfied by suits they often lose on appeal and which seldom vindicate their reputations because they do not establish the falsity of a story.

Annenberg's proposed Libel Reform Act recommends replacing costly, time-consuming libel litigation with a quick, low-cost procedure for determining whether or not a story was true. In the first stage of the dispute settlement, a person who claims to

---

[9]Newton v. NBC, 677 Fed. Supp. 1066, 14 Med. L. Rptr. 1914 (1987).

[10]*E.g.*,"$100 Million for GTE in Libel Case," *New York Times*, August 3, 1989, at 25.

[11]"The Verdict Is Libel, and the Trend Is Up," *New York Times*, March 11, 1988, at B11.

have been libeled would first seek a retraction or a chance to reply. If either is granted, the aggrieved person could not sue for damages.

However, if a media organization does not offer a retraction or an opportunity to reply, the person offended could sue. Under the Annenberg plan, either side in the dispute could require that the trial be limited to the question of the truth of the report rather than a question of monetary damages. Issues such as negligence or reckless disregard of the truth would not be factors in the case. The losing side would be required to pay the winner only attorneys' fees. If both sides of a dispute want to try a case for damages, the Annenberg proposal eliminates the chance of recovering punitive damages.

Media representatives criticize the Annenberg proposal for abandoning constitutional protection such as *New York Times* actual malice, even in return for protection against monetary damages. Media representatives also fear that state legislators enacting the Annenberg proposal into law would drop aspects more favorable to the media. "I don't trust legislatures," explained prominent media lawyer Floyd Abrams, who represented NBC in its suit against Wayne Newton.[12]

Media critics protested the Annenberg plan's virtual elimination of damage awards. Defense lawyer John Walsh, who represented former Mobil Oil President William Tavoulareas in his libel suit against the *Washington Post*, said the plan would provide no means of recovery for "businesses wiped out overnight" by false stories.[13]

Bills similar to the Annenberg proposal have failed in California, Connecticut, Iowa, and Illinois.

---

[12]Mauro, "The Annenberg Libel Plan," *Wash. Journalism Rev.*, April 1989, at 7.

[13]Id.

4
PRIVACY

The Supreme Court issued two major decisions affecting the law of privacy and emotional distress since *The Law of Public Communication* was published.   In one decision, the Court overturned a ruling punishing a newspaper for publishing the name of a rape victim. In the other, the Court held that *Hustler Magazine* is not liable to the Rev. Jerry Falwell for publishing a tasteless advertising parody that Falwell said inflicted emotional distress.

In decisions by other courts, comedian Woody Allen stopped advertisements by a celebrity look-alike, and a Tennessee court ruled Elvis Presley's estate controlled commercial rights to the late singer's personality.

PRIVATE FACTS

Public Records and Official Proceedings (pp. 172-174)

In June 1989, the U.S. Supreme Court reversed a judgment against *The Florida Star*, a weekly Jacksonville newspaper, for publishing the name of a rape victim in violation of a state statute. In *The Florida Star v. B.J.F.*, the Supreme Court ruled 6-3 that the First Amendment bars punishment of a newspaper for publication of lawfully obtained, truthful information unless punishment would further a government interest of the "highest order."[1]

In a narrow decision, the court reversed a Florida appeals court judgment against *The Star* for reporting the full name of B.J.F., a rape victim, in the paper's "Police Reports." The name was acquired by a reporter-trainee from a press release prepared by the Duval County Sheriff's Department and published in violation of the paper's own internal policy. A jury awarded B.J.F. $75,000 in compensatory damages and $25,000 in punitive damages for the paper's violation of the statute. The statute bars an "instrument of mass communication" from printing, publishing, or broadcasting the name of the victim of a sexual offense. A Florida appeals court affirmed the jury award, and the Florida Supreme Court refused review. The U.S. Supreme Court reversed.

The Star argued the U.S. Supreme Court's decision should be based on the Court's earlier ruling in *Cox Broadcasting Corp. v. Cohn*. In *Cox*, he Supreme Court held that the First Amendment bars media liability for invasion of privacy when the name of a rape victim is acquired from public court records (p. 172). *The Star* argued the press release from which the paper acquired B.J.F.'s name was a public record similar to court records from which the name of a rape victim was acquired in *Cox v. Cohn*. But in *B.J.F.*, the Supreme Court limited its *Cox* ruling to information acquired in open court. In a majority decision written by Justice Marshall, the Court in *B.J.F.* recognized a stronger First Amendment interest in reporting open court proceedings than in reporting from law enforcement records because the press traditionally has had a role ensuring the fairness of open trials.

The Court also refused in *B.J.F.*, as it did in *Cox*, to rule that the First Amendment protects publication of all truthful information. Marshall said the sensitive and significant interests presented in clashes between the First Amendment and privacy rights should be balanced in each case. Relying on an earlier decision in *Smith v. Daily Mail Publishing Co.* (pp. 419-420), the Court said the government may constitutionally punish a newspaper for publishing lawfully obtained, truthful information about a matter of public significance only if the government can show that punishment will "further a state interest of the highest order."

Applying the *Daily Mail* balancing test to the *B.J.F.* case, the Court determined that the weekly newspaper had lawfully obtained truthful information about a matter of public significance. The commission and investigation of violent crime, such as rape, is a subject of "paramount public import," the Court said. The newspaper lawfully acquired the name of the rape victim from a press release issued by the Sheriff's Department. If the government wishes to keep information confidential, the Court said, it should establish stronger safeguards on disclosure, not punish the press. Citizens hurt by dissemination of information released by the government should seek restitution from the government, not the media, the Court said. Indeed, the Duval County Sheriff's Department had earlier settled a civil suit with B.J.F. for $2,500.

---

[1] 57 U.S.L.W. 4816 (June 20, 1989).

Continuing his balancing analysis, Justice Marshall said that punishing *The Star* would not further the significant state interests in protecting rape victims' privacy and safety and encouraging them to report rapes without fear of exposure or reprisal. The Florida statute cannot be assumed to protect the privacy of a rape victim, the Court said, because it punishes publication of a victim's name in an "instrument of mass communication," but allows dissemination by other means, such as gossips or the victim herself. "When a State attempts the extraordinary measure of punishing truthful publication in the name of privacy, it must demonstrate its commitment to advancing this interest by applying its prohibition evenhandedly, to the smalltime disseminator as well as the media giant," the Court said.

The Court also objected because the Florida statute made the press liable whether or not the name was already public, regardless of whether publication was offensive to anyone, and without consideration of the publisher's motives. Such automatic liability, without case-by-case weighing of competing values, motives, and damages is unconstitutional where important First Amendment interests are at stake.

Justice Marshall was joined in his decision by Justices Brennan, Blackmun, and Stevens, and by the newest Reagan appointee, Justice Kennedy. Justice Scalia, also a recent Reagan appointee, wrote a concurring opinion.

Justice White filed a dissenting opinion in which he was joined by Chief Justice Rehnquist and Justice O'Connor. The dissenters feared that the Court's decision would "obliterate" liability for publication of private facts. "If the First Amendment prohibits wholly private persons (such as B.J.F.) from recovering for the publication of the fact that she was raped, I doubt that there remain any 'private facts' which persons may assume will not be published in the newspapers, or broadcast on television," Justice White said.

The dissenters found no public interest in publishing the names, addresses, and phone numbers of crime victims and no public interest in "immunizing the press from liability in the rare cases where a State's efforts to protect a victim's privacy have failed." The dissenters said that Florida had taken adequate safeguards to prohibit dissemination of B.J.F.'s full name. The room in which the Duval County Sheriff's Department released the victim's name contained signs warning that names of rape victims were not matters of public record.

The dissenters also dismissed the majority's concern about holding the media liable under a statute that punished only the mass media and failed to consider the intent of the publisher and the offensiveness of the revelation. The dissenters thought it proper to punish the media, but not individual gossips, because the Florida legislature determined that gossips do not pose the same danger of to rape victim's privacy as the mass media do. The dissenters also noted that the jury had determined *The Star* published B.J.F.'s name with "reckless indifference to the rights of others." Furthermore, the dissenters said the Florida legislature had appropriately determined that revelation of the name of a rape victim is categorically offensive.

Before the Supreme Court decided *Florida Star*, a California appeals court ruled that a crime witnesses' safety and the state's interest in conducting a criminal investigation might outweigh a newspaper's First Amendment interest in publishing the name of a crime witness. In a case that was later settled out of court, the California Court of Appeals denied summary judgment to the *Los Angeles Times* in a privacy suit over publication of the name of a woman who could identify a murder suspect still at large.[2] The woman, called Jane Doe in court papers, briefly saw the murderer of her roommate as he fled her apartment. Doe sued the Times-Mirror Company, publisher of the *Los Angeles Times*, for invasion of privacy, claiming the identification made her a target of the murderer.

The Times-Mirror Company argued that summary judgment should be granted because the First Amendment protects publication of newsworthy public information. Relying on *Hyde v. City of Columbia* (p. 184), the California Appeals Court denied summary judgment, concluding the First Amendment provides no absolute protection from liability for printing the name of a witness who can identify a murder suspect still at large. "The individual's safety and the state's interest in conducting a criminal investigation may take precedence over the public's right to know the name of the individual," the court said. Even if names appear on a public record, the court said, it does not mean "the press can print names in connection with sensitive information with impunity." The case was settled for an undisclosed sum after the U.S. Supreme Court refused review.[3]

In 1989, the North Carolina Supreme Court refused to recognize private facts claims. The Court said that the private facts branch of privacy law is "constitutionally suspect" and duplicates emotional distress claims which are recognized in North Carolina.[4] The Court thought it unlikely that a plaintiff claiming offensive publication of intimate facts could not as easily claim intentional infliction of emotional distress.

The North Carolina Supreme Court's decision reversed an appeals court's denial of summary judgment for the *The Salisbury Post*, a newspaper that published legally acquired names from adoption records. Adoption records are not public in North Carolina.[5]

EMOTIONAL DISTRESS

Intentional Infliction (pp. 181-183)

A Supreme Court ruling welcomed by the media in 1988 was the Court's decision that *Hustler Magazine* was not liable for an advertising parody that the Rev. Jerry Falwell

---

[2]Times-Mirror Co. v. San Diego Super. Ct., 2198 Cal. App.3d 1420, 744 Cal. Rptr. 556, 15 Med. L. Rptr. 1129 (1988).

[3]"Witness, *Times* Settle Privacy Suit," *News Media Update*, April 15, 1989, at 2.

[4]Hall v. Post, 15 Med. L. Rptr. 2329 (1988).

[5]Hall v. Post, 355 S.E.2d 818, 14 Med. L. Rptr. 1129 (N.C. App. 1987).

claimed inflicted emotional distress.[6] The advertisement portrayed a drunken Falwell having sex with his mother in an outhouse (see next page of the *Update*). Reversing the Fourth Circuit (pp. 182-183), a unanimous Supreme Court held in *Hustler Magazine, Inc. v. Falwell* that a public figure such as the Rev. Falwell cannot collect damages for emotional distress inflicted by a cartoon or caricature unless the publication contains false statements of fact that are published with malice as defined in *New York Times v. Sullivan*. The Court's decision means that public figures will seldom be able to sue successfully over even the most biting criticism unless it is defamatory and published with malice. Chief Justice Rehnquist, writing for a unanimous court, agreed with Falwell that the *Hustler* advertisement was "doubtless gross and repugnant in the eyes of most." But the ad was constitutionally protected because it contained ideas and opinions about a public figure.

Chief Justice Rehnquist looked to libel law for his reasoning. Rehnquist noted that the heart of the First Amendment is protection of the free flow of ideas and opinions on matters of public interest and concern. Even false defamatory statements about public officials and figures are protected if they are not published with "knowing falsehood or reckless disregard for the truth." Ideas and opinions are even more protected in public debate because there is no such thing as a false idea.

The caricature of Falwell in *Hustler* was constitutionally protected because it, too, contained ideas and opinions about a public figure. The ad did not contain "actual facts" about Falwell "or actual events in which [he] participated." The advertisement contained statements about Falwell that were so outrageous that they could not be true, and no one thought they were. The very outrageousness of the advertisement put it in the realm of ideas and opinion.

Falwell argued that he should collect damages, not because the parody was false, but because it was so offensively outrageous. However, the Court said an "outrageousness" standard of liability is unconstitutional as applied to public figures because it is too subjective and would punish the publisher's motives.

Rehnquist said public debate might suffer no harm if courts could punish outrageous cartoons, but the Chief Justice said he doubted there is any principled way to make a distinction between outrageous and reasonable cartoons. "'Outrageousness' in the area of political and social discourse," he said,

> has an inherent subjectiveness about it which would allow a jury to impose liability on the basis of the jurors' tastes or views, or perhaps on the basis of their dislike of a particular expression. An 'outrageousness' standard thus runs afoul of our longstanding refusal to allow damages to be awarded because the speech in question may have an adverse emotional impact on the audience."[7]

---

[6]Hustler Magazine, Inc. v. Falwell, 108 S. Ct. 876, 14 Med. L. Rptr. 2281 (1988).

[7]*Id.*, 108 S. Ct. at 882, 14 Med. L. Rptr. at 2285.

Jerry Falwell talks about his first time.*

FALWELL: My first time was in an outhouse outside Lynchburg, Virginia.

INTERVIEWER: Wasn't it a little cramped?

FALWELL: Not after I kicked the goat out.

INTERVIEWER: I see. You must tell me all about it.

FALWELL: I never *really* expected to make it with Mom, but then after she showed all the other guys in town such a good time, I figured, "What the hell!"

INTERVIEWER: But your mom? Isn't that a bit odd?

FALWELL: I don't think so. Looks don't mean that much to me in a woman.

INTERVIEWER: Go on.

FALWELL: Well, we were drunk off our God-fearing asses on Campari, ginger ale and soda—that's called a Fire and Brimstone—at the time. And Mom looked better than a Baptist whore with a $100 donation.

INTERVIEWER: Campari in the crapper with Mom . . . how interesting. Well, how was it?

FALWELL: The Campari was great, but Mom passed out before I could come.

INTERVIEWER: Did you ever try it again?

FALWELL: Sure . . .

lots of times. But not in the outhouse. Between Mom and the shit, the flies were too much to bear.

INTERVIEWER: We meant the Campari.

FALWELL: Oh, yeah. I always get sloshed before I go out to the pulpit. You don't think I could lay down all that bullshit *sober*, do you?

© 1983—Imported by Campari U.S.A. New York, NY 48°proof Spirit Aperitif (Liqueur)

Campari, like all liquor, was made to mix you up. It's a light, 48-proof, refreshing spirit, just mild enough to make you drink too much before you know you're schnockered. For your first time, mix it with orange juice. Or maybe some white wine. Then you won't remember anything the next morning. **Campari. *The mixable that smarts.***

CAMPARI You'll never forget your first time.

*AD PARODY—NOT TO BE TAKEN SERIOUSLY

(Reproduced with permission of L.F.P. Inc., and Larry Flynt.)

The Court also said that holding Larry Flynt, publisher of *Hustler*, liable for "outrageous" political opinions would unconstitutionally punish him for bad motives. In debate about public affairs, the Court said, the First Amendment protects many things "done with motives that are less than admirable." Indeed, the Court noted, a political cartoon is often "intentionally injurious;" the purpose of a political cartoon is to be "a weapon of attack, of scorn and ridicule and satire." In other words, the cartoonist's motive is to be outrageous.

Political cartoons, by their nature, frequently go beyond the bounds of good taste and manners. The Court said the *Hustler* cartoon was a tasteless version of political cartoons that have flayed public figures throughout American history. Justice Rehnquist compared the advertising parody to political cartoons of Thomas Nast, which castigated the Tweed Ring in New York, and to cartoons of George Washington portrayed as an ass. Cartoons may be offensive, but they contain constitutionally protected ideas and opinion.

For a public official or public figure to collect damages for intentional infliction of emotional distress, the Court said the publication must, like defamation, contain a false statement and be published with malice. There was no falsity in the *Hustler* ad, the Court said, because no one believed the preposterous statements about the Rev. Falwell.

INTRUSION AND TRESPASS

Intrusion into Private Places (p. 189)

The Iowa Supreme Court in 1987 ruled that a restaurant might be a sufficiently secluded place that a patron could sue the media for unwanted filming there. The Iowa court ruled Theresa Stessman had a cause of action against the American Black Hawk Broadcasting Company for filming her despite her objection as she dined in a public restaurant.[8] In allowing the suit to proceed, the court said filming a person in a private dining room "might conceivably be a highly offensive intrusion upon that person's seclusion." The court said there was no evidence that Stessman was secluded in the restaurant, but there was no evidence she was not. With a factual question to be answered, the court refused summary judgment for the broadcaster.

However, a federal court in Maine ruled that a *National Enquirer* reporter did not intrude when she persistently sought interviews with Henry Dempsey at his home and at a restaurant.[9] The reporter also tried to photograph Dempsey at the restaurant. The court said it is not intrusive to attempt to take a photograph in a restaurant open to the public. The court also noted that the *Enquirer* reporter did not attempt to enter Dempsey's house. The reporter's attempts to get an interview may have been "annoying," the court said, but they were not "highly offensive" and therefore did not constitute intrusion.

---

[8]Stessman v. American Black Hawk Broadcasting Co., 416 N.W.2d 685, 14 Med. L. Rptr. 2073 (1987).

[9]Dempsey v. National Enquirer, 16 Med. L. Rptr. 1396 (D. Maine 1988).

Participant Monitoring (pp. 190-191)

In August 1988, a federal district court in Ohio reaffirmed that federal law permits one
party to record a conversation without telling the other party.[10] The federal court
dismissed a case brought by Sandra Boddie against ABC for secretly taping an interview
with her. Boddie had agreed to be interviewed off camera by Geraldo Rivera for a
segment of "20/20" about a judge who traded light criminal sentences for sex. But ABC
secretly taped the conversation with Boddie, an alleged participant in the scandal.

Boddie claimed the taped interview violated the federal wiretap statute that barred
recording without telling all parties if the recording were for the purpose of "committing
any criminal or tortious act" or "committing any other injurious act." Boddie claimed the
interview, which was broadcast, was intentionally designed to injure her.

A federal circuit court ruled in 1984 that Boddie might pursue her case in court.
However, Congress, in 1986, repealed the clause in the wiretap statute that permitted a
party to a secretly recorded conversation to sue for recordings made "for the purpose of
committing any other injurious act." In 1988, the federal district court in Ohio dismissed
Boddie's privacy claim, saying that Congress never intended the wiretap statute to bar
the media from secretly recording interviews unless the media planned some criminal or
tortious use of the tape, such as blackmail, threats, or public embarrassment.

Trespass

Accompanying Officials (pp. 196-198)

A California appeals court in 1987 joined an increasing number of courts ruling that
journalists may be liable for accompanying officials into private places. The Court of
Appeal for the Second District held in *Miller v. National Broadcasting Company* that Ms.
Brownie Miller had a cause of action for trespass, intrusion, and infliction of emotional
distress against a Los Angeles television news crew that accompanied paramedics on an
emergency mission to Miller's home.[11] KNBC, which was preparing a documentary on
paramedics, accompanied a unit of paramedics into Miller's home the night her husband
suffered a heart attack. Miller, who was in a different room, was not aware that the
media were in her home, but learned of the entry when NBC broadcast the paramedics'
unsuccessful attempt to save her husband.

In recognizing the legitimacy of Miller's intrusion claim, the court said journalists,
like most individuals, may not go into private homes without consent of the householder
unless the journalist is acting in some official capacity. Reasonable people, the court

---

[10]Boddie v. American Broadcasting Companies, Inc., 694 F. Supp. 1304, 16 Med. L. Rptr.
1100 (N.D. Ohio 1988), *aff'd*, 16 Med.L. Rptr. 2038 (6th Cir. 1989).

[11]187 Cal. App. 3d 1463, 232 Cal. Rptr. 668 (1987).

said, could regard the NBC camera crew's intrusion into Mr. Miller's bedroom "at a time of vulnerability and confusion occasioned by his seizure as 'highly offensive' conduct."[12]

FALSE LIGHT (pp. 199-200)

The media won several false light cases in the last two years either because the law did not recognize the false light tort or because the plaintiff did not establish a false statement of fact. Courts in Ohio,[13] Kentucky,[14] and the District of Columbia[15] refused to recognize the tort of false light invasion of privacy.

Distortion (pp. 200-202)

The Oregon Court of Appeals ruled that a trial should be held to determine whether a newspaper photo taken at the public opening of an alcohol rehabilitation center falsely portrayed a man as a patient at the center.[16] A picture in the *Eugene Register Guard* showed Orlin Dean with nurses in the center's "aversion treatment" room during an open house. Dean, an admitted alcoholic, said the picture falsely portrayed him as a patient receiving treatment to make alcohol unappealing to him. The newspaper argued that the photograph did not imply that Dean was a patient. The paper also argued that Dean had no false light claim even if the picture did imply he was a patient because there is nothing offensive about a known alcoholic seeking treatment.

A lower court ruled for the newspaper. But the appeals court reversed and remanded the case for trial to determine if it was reasonable for an alcoholic to be highly offended if he were falsely portrayed as a patient receiving aversion treatment.

COMMERCIALIZATION

Appropriation

Trade Purposes (pp. 209-210)

The U.S. District Court for the District of Rhode Island ruled in February 1988 that George Mendonsa, who claims to be the sailor in a famous Alfred Eisenstadt photo,

---

[12]*See generally*, Middleton, *Journalists, Trespass, and Officials: Closing the Door on Florida Publishing Co. v. Fletcher*, 16 Pepperdine L. Rev. 259 (1989).

[13]Angelotta v. American broadcasting Companies, Inc., 820 F.2d 806 (6th Cir. 1987).

[14]J. & C. Inc. v. Combined Communications Corp., 14 Med. L. Rptr. 2162 (Ky. Ct. App. 1987).

[15]Southern Air Transport, Inc. v. American Broadcasting Companies, Inc., 670 F. Supp. 38, 14 Med. L. Rptr. 1683 (D.C.D.C. 1987).

[16]Dean v. Guard Publishing Co., 744 P.2d 1296, 14 Med. L. Rptr. 2100 (Or. Ct. App. 1987).

could sue for unauthorized commercial use of his photo by Time, Inc., publisher of *Life Magazine*.[17] Mendonsa says he is the man in the Eisenstadt photo of a sailor kissing a nurse in New York City's Times Square moments after the announcement of the Japanese surrender in 1945. The photo first appeared in the August 27, 1945, edition of *Life*.

The original photo of Mendonsa in *Life* was not an unauthorized commercial use of Mendonsa's likeness because the photo was newsworthy. However, the court said Mendonsa might have an appropriation suit for later commercial use of the photo, particularly Time, Inc.'s recent attempt to sell the photograph in a limited edition for $1,600.

Defenses

Newsworthiness (pp. 210-212)

The New York Supreme Court ruled that broadcast of a "classic advertisement" in an entertainment program about great advertisements is a newsworthy use. The court therefore dismissed the complaint brought under the New York Civil Rights Statute by Charles C. Welch, an actor in the ad. Welch appeared in a Philip Morris advertisement in the 1960s that was one of four domestic "classic" ads inducted in 1986 into the "Clio Hall of Fame." Portions of the Philip Morris ad were broadcast in a *PM Magazine* segment about the "Clio Awards," which are annual awards for the best television advertisements.[18]

The New York court ruled that Welch's picture was not used for advertising or trade purposes in the *PM Magazine* broadcast. The broadcast segment contained no solicitation and promoted the sale of no product, the court said. On the contrary, the court said the segment was an educational presentation of the history of television commercials, which is a newsworthy subject.

The New York Supreme Court also ruled a newspaper may use a previously published picture in advertisements soliciting subscriptions.[19] The court ruled it was not a violation of the New York Civil Rights Statute for the *Village Voice* to use a previously published cover photo of Ramon Velez, a Hispanic activist, in a subscription advertisement. A cartoon balloon in the ad had Velez asking readers, "What's your address?" and directing them to a subscription coupon.

The New York court said reproduction of a newsworthy cover to promote a magazine is a "logical extension of the clearly protected editorial use of the content of the publication." Velez might bring a successful appropriation suit, the court suggested, if the newspaper promotion indicated that Velez endorsed the publication. But the cartoon

---

[17]Mendonsa v. Time, Inc., 678 F. Supp. 967, 15 Med. L. Rptr. 1017 (D.R.I. 1988).

[18]Welch v. Group W Productions, 138 Misc.2d 856, 525 N.Y.S.2d 466, 15 Med. L. Rptr. 1062 (S. Ct. 1987).

[19]Velez v. VV Publishing Corp., 135 A.D.2d 47, 524 N.Y.S.2d 186, 14 Med. L. Rptr. 2290 (1988).

balloon--"What's your address?--indicated fiction or satire, the court said, not endorsement. The court did not think a reasonable reader could take Velez' inquiry about addresses seriously. The fact that the *Voice* published the entire cover also indicated that Velez had not been hired to endorse the publication, the court said.

Right of Publicity (pp. 215-216)

The Utah Supreme Court ruled that Senator Orin Hatch did not violate the privacy of constituents by using their pictures in campaign literature.[20] Postal workers who posed with the senator argued he violated their rights of publicity by using the photos in his reelection campaign. The postal workers said use of their pictures constituted an implicit endorsement of the senator, which they did not intend.

The Utah court ruled that the campaign literature was newsworthy information protected by the First Amendment. Because of the First Amendment privilege, the court held that "pictures of public officials and candidates for public office taken in public or semi-public places with persons who either pose with them or who inadvertently appear in such pictures may not be made the basis for an invasion of privacy or abuse of personal identity action."

Furthermore, the court ruled that the postal workers had no appropriation claim because Hatch took nothing of value from them when he used their picture in his campaign literature. A political endorsement by an unknown member of the general public has no "intrinsic value," the court said. In addition, the court said the workers had no appropriation claim because use of their names and likenesses was "incidental to the purpose of showing Senator Hatch in the company of workers. Other workers' pictures would have sufficed as well."

Identification (pp. 216-218)

Early in 1988, the film director and comedian Woody Allen was granted an injunction to stop a clothing store from using an Allen look-alike in an ad, even though a disclaimer said the man in the ad was a celebrity look-alike. The U.S. District Court for the Southern District of New York enjoined Men's World Outlet, a discount clothier, and its advertising agency, Ribaudo & Schaefer, Inc., from publishing an ad containing a photograph of Allen look-alike Phil Boroff holding a clarinet. The copy evoked Allen's "schlemiel" personna."[21]

The court granted the injunction for Allen under the Lanham Act (p. 339) rather than the New York privacy statute. The court said readers of the ad might mistakenly think Allen endorsed clothes for Men's World.

The Men's World ad, which ran in *Newsweek*, was unusual because it contained a small disclaimer in light type stating that the man in the ad was a celebrity look-alike.

---

[20]Cox v. Hatch, 16 Med. L. Rptr. 1366 (Utah 1988).

[21]Allen v. Men's World Outlet, 679 F. Supp. 360, 15 Med. L. Rptr. 1001 (1988).

But the court said the disclaimer was too small to prevent confusion. The court also said the ad should contain a second disclaimer indicating that Allen did not endorse products for Men's World.

In a "sound-alike" case, a federal court in California ruled that a trial should be held on singer Bette Midler's appropriation claim. Midler claimed that the Ford Motor Company and the advertising agency, Young & Rubicam, Inc., appropriated her identity by broadcasting automobile advertisements with a singer who sounded like Midler. Several people testified that they thought Midler was singing her famous song, "Do You Want To Dance," in the commercials.[22]

The Ninth Circuit, overturning a lower court's grant of summary judgment, held it is a tort in California when advertisers deliberately imitate the distinctive voice of a widely known professional singer in order to sell a product. To impersonate a singer, the court said, "is to pirate her identity." Young & Rubicam had acquired permission to use the song, but not to imitate Midler's voice.

Descendibility (pp. 218-219)

The Tennessee Court of Appeals ruled in a case involving Elvis Presley's right of publicity that Tennessee common law permits a celebrity to leave intangible property rights to one's heirs.[23] In its ruling that Presley's publicity rights are descendible, the Tennessee court rejected the reasoning of the U.S. Court of Appeals for the Sixth Circuit. In 1980, the Sixth Circuit had ruled that Tennessee law does not recognize a right of publicity after death (p. 219).[24] The Tennessee Court of Appeals concluded that the Sixth Circuit's opinion was "based upon an incorrect construction of Tennessee law and is inconsistent with the better reasoned decisions in this field."

Shortly after the Tennessee ruling, the Sixth Circuit accepted the state court's interpretation of the common law of publicity.[25] The Sixth Circuit said it could not reject an interpretation of state law by a state appellate court unless there was an indication that the state supreme court would decide otherwise. The Sixth Circuit doubted the Tennessee Supreme Court would disagree with the appeals court's ruling that celebrity rights are descendible.

---

[22]Midler v. Ford Motor Co., 849 F.2d 460, 15 Med. L. Rptr. 1620 (9th Cir. 1988).

[23]Tennessee *ex rel.* Presley v. Crowell, 733 S.W.2d 89, 14 Med. L. Rptr. 1043 (Tenn. App. 1987).

[24]Memphis Development Foundation v. Factors Etc., Inc., 616 F.2d 956 (6th Cir. 1980), *cert. denied*, 449 U.S. 953 (1980). (The first printing of the textbook mistakenly says on page 219 that the Sixth Circuit Court was interpreting Kentucky law. The text should have said the court was interpreting Tennessee law.)

[25]Elvis Presley Enterprises v. Elvisly Yours, 817 F.2d 104, 14 Med. L. Rptr. 1053 (6th Cir. 1987).

5
INTELLECTUAL PROPERTY

In 1988, the United States joined the Berne Convention, the strongest international agreement for protecting intellectual property. As a result, notice requirements are no longer mandatory to protect copyright and the move towards recognition of moral rights continues. The 100th Congress also passed legislation that affects registration of trademarks, delivery of broadcasting to rural satellite dishes, and comparative advertisements. In June 1989, the Supreme Court resolved a judicial conflict over whether free-lance writers and other independent contractors are "employees."

COPYRIGHT

Copyrightable Works (pp. 224-226)

Two federal courts have ruled that editing techniques and frequently used devices in television productions may be copyrighted. In one case, a federal court in Minnesota refused summary judgment for a broadcast advertiser charged with violating another advertiser's copyright by employing the same actress and editing techniques.[1] In refusing to grant summary judgment, the court said there was substantial similarity between the ads, both of which were brief, rapidly paced spots employing Deborah Shelton of the television series "Dallas." While the use of Deborah Shelton could not be copyrighted, the combination of artistic choices--such as the composition of each frame,

---

[1]C. Blore & Don Richman, Inc. v. 20/20 Advertising Inc., 674 F. Supp. 671 (D. Minn. 1987).

pace of editing, camera angle, choice of actors and actresses, hairstyle, jewelry, decor, and makeup--could be, the court said.

In another case, a federal court in New York ruled that the original selection, organization, and presentation of frequently used devices in a television show are also copyrightable. The district court refused summary judgment in a suit in which producers of the television show, "To Tell the Truth," claimed copyright infringement by the show, "Bamboozle."[2] Both shows involve celebrities guessing which one of several panelists' stories is true. The court noted that none of the elements of the game shows can be copyrighted individually, not the idea of a show in which people lie, nor the use of contestants to guess who is lying. Neither can the use of celebrity guests, the system of asking questions, nor the employment of a master of ceremonies be copyrighted. But, the court said, the combination of these often-used devices can be protected. It is the "original selection, organization, and presentation" of these stock devices that are copyrightable.

Formalities

Notice (pp. 226-227)

In the fall of 1988, the U.S. agreed to join the Berne Convention for the Protection of Literary and Artistic Works.[3] American publishers and producers of films, records, and tapes hope that American membership in the Berne Convention, the strongest international copyright agreement, will dissuade other countries from pirating American works. Unauthorized copying of American productions, particularly in the Far East, is estimated to cost copyright holders $1.3 billion annually.[4]

The most significant change in U.S. law resulting from the Berne Convention Implementation Act is the abolition of the copyright notice requirement. After the Berne Convention took effect in the United States on March 1, 1989, all American and foreign authors in countries belonging to the convention enjoy copyright protection whether or not their works display a notice of copyright. A work no longer passes into the public domain if it is published without notice. Infringers may be enjoined or held liable for damages for violating the copyright of works containing no notice.

While notice is no longer required, placing notice on copyrighted works is still advisable. Notice deters would-be infringers by warning them that copyright is claimed. Furthermore, an infringer is barred from claiming "innocent" infringement of works bearing a copyright notice.

---

[2]Barris/Fraser Enterprises v. Goodson-Todman Enterprises Ltd., 35 *Pat., Trademark & Copyright J.* (BNA) 280 (Feb. 11, 1988).

[3]Berne Convention Implementation Act of 1988, Pub. L. 100-568, 102 Stat. 2854 (Oct. 31, 1988).

[4]"Two Worst Copyright Pirates Are China and Saudi Arabia, Report Says," 37 *Pat., Copyright & Trademark J.* (BNA) 673 (April 27, 1989). The report was published by the International Intellectual Property Alliance.

The new law implementing the Berne Convention also doubles the "statutory" damages a copyright owner may receive from an infringer without proving that the infringement caused financial loss. Under the new law, registration of copyright with the copyright office is still a prerequisite for American authors filing an infringement suit and claiming statutory damages and attorney's fees.

Copyright Ownership

Employer's Work Made for Hire (pp. 229-230)

The Supreme Court in 1989 resolved conflicts in the courts over when free-lance artists, writers, and photographers are "employees" of the hiring party. The Court ruled in *Community for Creative Non-Violence v. Reid* that free-lance artists and writers are "employees" of a hiring party only in those rare circumstances in which they meet the criteria of "employee" in the common law of "agency."[5] The law of agency determines relationships between "masters" and "servants" or "employees." The Court pointed out that the work-for-hire doctrine in which employers own copyright in the work of their "employees" carries "profound significance for free-lance creators--including artists, writers, photographers, designers, composers, and computer programmers--and for the publishing, advertising, music, and other industries which commission their works."

In *Community for Creative Non-Violence*, the Court ruled that James Earl Reid, a Baltimore sculptor, was not an employee of the Community, a non-profit association dedicated to eliminating homelessness. The Community had commissioned Reid to create a sculpture of a homeless family huddled on a steam grate. The Community claimed to be Reid's employer and sole copyright owner of the sculpture because the community "wielded control" over the project by conceiving the idea for the sculpture, engaging Reid to create the figures, and monitoring the artist's progress.

The Supreme Court, however, ruled that an employer-employee relationship is not created solely by the exercise of control over a free-lance artist or writer. Determining copyright ownership by the degree of supervision, the Court said, was not the intent of Congress in passing copyright legislation and would deny creators the predictability that copyright law is supposed to ensure. If degree of supervision determines employment and copyright ownership, the Court said, a creator might not know who owned copyright until after a work was completed.

Relying on the law of agency, the Supreme Court ruled that an employer-employee relationship is determined by several factors, none of them determinative itself. One of the factors is the degree of the hiring party's supervision over the work. But several other factors must also be considered, such as the skill required of the creator, the source of the tools, the location of the work, the duration of the relationship between the parties, the creator's discretion over when and how long to work, and the provision of employee benefits.

---

[5] 57 U.S.L.W. 4607.

Although the Community for Creative Non-Violence monitored Reid's work, the Supreme Court ruled Reid was an independent contractor, not an employee, because he was a skilled professional who supplied his own tools, worked in his own studio, and had only a short-term business relationship with the committee. Furthermore, the Community had no right to assign additional projects to Reid, had no authority to tell Reid when to work, had no discretion over the hiring and paying of Reid's assistants, and did not pay social security and payroll taxes or provide employee benefits. The Court said that the sculpture, to which the Community contributed the steam grate, might be a joint work, but was not work for hire made by an employee.

The Court's decision means that a work for hire falls into two categories, those created in an employer-employee relationship as defined in *Community for Creative Non-Violence*, and works commissioned for a newspaper, magazine, or news program, when a written contract says that the work is a work for hire. If there is no employer-employee relationship and no work-for-hire contract for a commissioned work, copyright belongs to the creator unless the parties voluntarily make some other arrangement.

Thus, if the Travenol Laboratories case (p. 229) were brought today, the drug company probably would not own copyright in the newsletter printed and distributed by an advertising agency. Similarly, the handbook written by a volunteer for the Town of Clarkston (p. 230) would probably belong to the author, not to the town. Likewise, videotapes of the New Orleans Mardi Gras would likely belong to the television station that produced them, not to the organization that commissioned them (p. 230).[6] Newspapers, too, would probably not be "employees" of merchants who commission the papers to create advertisements (p. 230).

Community for Creative Non-Violence may encourage publishers and others to claim copyright ownership as "joint authors" in free-lance work. A hiring party that contributes original expression to a free-lance work may claim joint ownership in the whole work. The federal appeals court in Washington suggested that the Community's contribution of the steam grate on which Reid's sculpted figures sat could make the Community a joint author--and therefore a joint copyright owner--in the entire sculpture. Editors, advertising agencies, and others who hire free-lance workers might also claim joint authorship if they actively participate in writing, composing, and editing free-lance work.

---

[6]In *Community for Creative Non-Violence*, the Supreme Court agreed with a federal appeals court ruling that copyright in tapes of the New Orleans Mardi Gras belong to WYES, the station that made the tapes, not the Easter Seal Society, the organization that requested the tapes. The appeals court said the station owned the tapes, not because the Easter Seal Society failed to supervise the production, but because the station, as an independent contractor, was not an "employee." Easter Seal Soc'y for Crippled Children and Adults of Louisiana, Inc. v. Playboy Enterprises, 815 F.2d 323 (5th Cir. 1987), *cert. denied*, 108 S. Ct. 1280 (1988). A federal district court had ruled that the station owned the tapes because the Easter Seal Society failed to supervise the production (p. 230).

Rights

Performance and Display

Cable (pp. 234-235) The 100th Congress passed a law in October 1988 that allows households in remote places to receive network and super station programming via satellite. The Satellite Home Viewer Act of 1988 creates a six-year license for households in areas not served by over-the-air broadcasting to pull network and super station programs from satellites.[7]

The satellite act does not allow homeowners in rural areas to watch satellite transmissions intended for distribution by cable systems. In fact, the act creates new penalties for pirating cable signals beamed by satellite. Under the act, pirating of cable transmissions or manufacture and sale of illegal receivers for cable signals could result in fines up to $50,000 and two years in prison for the first offense.

Copying (pp. 236-237)

The U.S. Court of Appeals for the Ninth Circuit ruled that a contract permitting use of a copyrighted work in one medium does not extend to new technologies.[8] The Ninth Circuit ruled that Paramount Pictures Corporation infringed the copyright on the song "Merry-Go-Round" by copying and distributing videotapes of the film "Medium Cool" in which the song appeared. Under a license agreed to in 1969, Paramount had the right to distribute the film with the song in movie theaters and to exhibit it on television. However, the 1969 license did not give Paramount the right to make and sell videocassettes of the movie, the court said. In the contract, the copyright owner retained all rights except for performance of the song when the film was shown in theaters and on television.

Paramount argued that selling the videocassettes was no different than exhibiting the film on television as the original contract allowed. But the court ruled that the copyright holder in 1969 could not have considered videocassettes to be like television broadcasts because videocassettes were not yet invented or envisioned. "We would frustrate the purpose of the [Copyright] Act," the court said, "were we to construe this license--with its limiting language--as granting a right in a medium that had not been introduced to the domestic market at the time the parties entered into the agreement."

Moral Rights (p. 237-238)

The United States joined the Berne Convention for the Protection of Literary and Artistic Works so that copyright in American films and books could be better protected abroad. But the U.S. agreed to join the convention only after American publishers and art dealers were satisfied that signing the accord would not add new moral rights requirements to

---

[7]Pub. L. 100-667 (Nov. 16, 1988).

[8]Cohen v. Paramount Pictures Corp., 7 U.S.P.Q.2d 1570 (1988).

United States copyright law.[9] American publishers and art dealers were afraid that membership in Berne might require them to limit editing, ensure that works were not altered, and give artists part of the profits as works were sold and resold. The Berne Convention requires member nations to protect the moral rights of artists in their work.

The U.S. was able to join the Berne Convention without adding moral rights. Signatories of the convention may recognize moral rights in their own way, including through the laws of defamation, privacy, and unfair competition, laws that are already well-developed in the U.S.

Although the U.S. did not add moral rights provisions to its copyright law, the Copyright Office in March 1989 recommended that Congress "seriously consider a unified system of moral rights."[10] The Copyright Office followed the urgings of film directors, screenwriters, and actors who object to colorization of black a nd white films, editing of films for television schedules, and "panning" to adapt wide-screen films to smaller video screens.

In September 1988, President Reagan signed a law requiring that distinguished films on a new National Film Registry be labeled if they are altered. The new law, the National Film Preservation Act, establishes a 13-member National Film Preservation Board that will select up to 25 significant films each year for inclusion on the national registry.[11] Films that are "culturally, historically, or aesthetically significant" may be selected for the registry 10 years after their release. Under terms of the act, registered black-and-white films must be labeled if they are colorized or otherwise materially altered.

Fair Use (pp. 238-239)

A federal district court ruled in 1987 that a trial should be held to determine whether an advertiser violates copyright and trademark by quoting a consumer magazine's favorable product evaluation. The federal district court refused to grant summary judgment to The New Regina Corporation and its advertising agency in a copyright suit over vacuum cleaner advertisements quoting *Consumer Reports*.[12] Consumers Union, publisher of *Consumer Reports*, charged that Regina violated the publisher's copyright and trademark by quoting the magazine's positive rating of the Powerteam vacuum in a television advertisement.

---

[9]"House Unanimously Passes Berne Implementation Legislation," 36 *Pat., Copyright & Trademark J.* (BNA) 25 (May 12, 1988).

[10]Film Alteration Report Recommends Consideration of Moral Rights System," 37 *Pat., Copyright & Trademark J.* (BNA) 498 (March 16, 1989).

[11]Pub. L. 100-446, 2 U.S.C. 178.

[12]Consumers Union of United States, Inc. v. New Regina Corp., 664 F. Supp. 753 (S.D.N.Y. 1987).

Earlier, a federal appeals court lifted an injunction to allow ads for the Regina Elictrikbroom Powerteam HB 6910 to be broadcast (pp. 224 and 243).[13] On remand, the U.S. District Court for the Southern District of New York refused to stop the litigation because, it said, questions about fair use and trademark violations need to be tried in court. The federal district court, in a four-part analysis of fair use, said the vacuum cleaner advertisements appropriated the most significant portion of *Consumer Reports'* product research and used it for a commercial purpose. Harm is presumed, the court noted, where copyrighted expression is used for commercial purposes.

Most important to the court, however, was the effect the advertisement might have on *Consumer Reports'* potential market (p. 248). Consumers Union claimed that the public would lose confidence in the organization's neutrality if manufacturers could associate Consumers Union with advertised products by routinely publishing its evaluations. Circulation of *Consumer Reports* would decline as public confidence waned, Consumers Union argued.

The federal district court ruled Consumers Union should have an opportunity to present evidence that quotations from *Consumer Reports'* product evaluations in advertisements would diminish consumer confidence and the magazine's circulation. The district court also said a trial should be held to determine if use of the *Consumer Reports'* trademark in product advertisements would cause consumers to mistakenly believe that Consumers Union approved of the products. This consumer confusion would violate the Lanham Trademark Act, Consumers Union said.

UNFAIR COMPETITION

Misappropriation (pp. 252-253)

A federal appeals court in New York ruled that the idea for "The Cosby Show" was not original and therefore could not be protected from misappropriation.[14] The loser in the case was Hwesu S. Murray who, while an NBC employee in 1980, submitted a proposal to create a half-hour situation comedy starring Bill Cosby. Like "The Cosby Show," which premiered four years later, Murray's proposal focused on a closely-knit black family headed by a compassionate, proud father. After acquiring more details from Murray, NBC told him the network was not interested in producing the show. When "The Cosby Show" appeared in 1984, Murray sued under several branches of business law for appropriation of his idea without compensation.

The U.S. Court of Appeals for the Second Circuit said that NBC's "The Cosby Show" is a breakthrough because it portrays blacks in a more positive, fair, and realistic manner than before. But the idea of portraying a happy, well-to-do, black family was not

---

[13]Consumers Union of United States, Inc. v. General Signal Corp., 724 F.2d 1044 (2d Cir. 1983), *cert. denied*, 469 U.S. 823 (1984).

[14]Murray v. NBC, 844 F.2d 988, 15 Med. L. Rptr. 1284 (2d Cir. 1988).

original to Murray, the court said. Besides, the court observed, Bill Cosby had long said publicly he wished to create a situation comedy peopled with middle-class blacks.

Trademark Infringement (pp. 253-254)

Congress in late 1988 passed a major revision of the trademark law. The Trademark Law Revision Act of 1988 revises provisions in the Lanham Act regulating registration of trademarks and their use in advertising.[15] The revision affecting advertising is discussed in Chapter 7.

Under the new law, which went into effect in November 1989, companies no longer have to use a trademark in commerce before registering it with the Patent and Trademark Office in Washington, D.C. Under the new law, companies no longer have to develop, distribute, and promote a new product before claiming--and perhaps being denied--trademark registration.

The trademark revision law still allows companies to register a mark after using it in commerce, but companies may also receive provisional approval before using the mark if they demonstrate a "bona fide intention" to use the mark within six months. Once the mark is used in commerce, the Patent and Trademark Office will issue a registration certificate. Under the new law, registration must be renewed every 10 years instead of every 20 as under previous law.

The Trademark Law Revision Act also adds a new section that protects famous trademarks, such as Kodak and Buick, from "dilution." Protection against dilution does not assume that a consumer will be confused or deceived, but that the uniqueness and aura of a famous mark will be diluted by use on dissimilar products. The new section, 43(c), protects famous trademarks from unauthorized use on dissimilar products such as Kodak pianos or Buick aspirin. The new law provides consistent national protection for extremely valuable famous marks. Before revision of the federal trademark law, 23 states had dilution laws.[16]

Inherently Distinctive Marks (pp. 254-255)

The U.S. Court of Appeals for the Seventh Circuit ruled in 1989 that "LA" is a descriptive mark for low alcohol beer and therefore is not protected under the Lanham Trademark Act.[17] In a ruling against Anheuser-Busch, the court agreed that G. Heileman Brewing Company and other brewers could use the "LA" designation on their light beers. By ruling that "LA" is not a distinctive mark, the Seventh Circuit disagrees with the U.S. Court of Appeals for the Eighth Circuit, which ruled that "LA" is a distinctive mark belonging to Anheuser-Busch (p. 255).

---

[15]Pub. L. 100-667.

[16]See, S. Rep. No. 100-515, 100th Cong., 2d Sess. 7, reprinted in 1988 U.S. Code Cong. & Ad. News 5577, 5583-84.

[17]G. Heileman Brewing Co. v. Anheuser-Busch, Inc., 38 Pat., Trademark & Copyright J. (BNA) 34 (7th Cir. May 11, 1989).

Rejecting Anheuser-Busch's claim that "LA" "suggests" light beer without actually describing it, the Seventh Circuit said the "L" and the "A" are merely initials that describe the low alcohol content of the beer. Furthermore, the court saw no danger of confusion among consumers if several companies use the "LA" designation. Confusion would not occur, the court said, because beer companies also put their names on the labels.

Infringement (pp. 256-257)

The U.S. Court of Appeals for the Second Circuit has ruled that *ADWEEK's Marketing Week*, published by an American firm, infringed the trademark of the British publication, *Marketing Week*.[18] The court ruled that although *Marketing Week* was not inherently distinctive, it had acquired a distinct identity or secondary meaning (p. 255) during nearly 10 years of sales to a small group of international marketers. The court was most convinced of the secondary meaning of *Marketing Week* by *ADWEEK*'s deliberate copying of *Marketing Week*'s mark.

---

[18]Centaur Communications, Ltd. v. A/S/M Communications, Inc., 830 F.2d 1217 (1987).

6
CORPORATE SPEECH

The Supreme Court delivered several opinions during the last two years affecting corporate and union expression. One decision permits a company to pay people to gather names for a referendum petition. Another permits union handbilling and a third defines when information about a proposed corporate merger becomes "material." The Court also upheld the conviction of a *Wall Street Journal* reporter who traded on information he knew was going to be published in the newspaper. Congress passed legislation to curb insider trading.

REFERENDA AND PUBLIC ISSUES

Corporate and Citizen Rights

Corporate Right to Speak and Publish (pp. 264-265)

In 1988, the Supreme Court extended the First Amendment rights of corporations to spend money in referenda. In *Meyer v. Grant*,[1] the Court held that corporations--or anyone else--may hire professionals to gather signatures to place a proposal on the ballot. The Court's ruling, which affirmed a lower court decision, struck down a Colorado law that made it a felony to pay petition circulators.

Under Colorado law, as under the law in many states, proponents of a new law or constitutional amendment may have their proposal placed on the ballot in a general election if they obtain a prescribed number of signatures on an "initiative petition." However, to preserve the integrity of the referendum process, the Colorado legislature

---

[1]108 S. Ct. 1887 (1988).

prohibited payment for gathering signatures. The statute was challenged by truckers seeking deregulation from government controls. The truckers wanted to pay professional solicitors to gather signatures so that Colorado voters might choose to remove motor carriers from the jurisdiction of the Colorado Public Utilities Commission.

The Supreme Court unanimously struck down the section of the Colorado law prohibiting payment for solicitation of signatures. The circulation of a petition, Justice Stevens wrote for the Court, involves "interactive communication concerning political change that is appropriately described as 'core political speech.'" Whether the trucking industry should be deregulated in Colorado is a matter of societal concern that the industry has a right to discuss publicly, the Court said. Furthermore, the Court said, "circulation of an initiative petition of necessity involves both the expression of a desire for political change and a discussion of the merits of the proposed change."

The Court said the Colorado prohibition of payments to petition circulators unconstitutionally restricted political expression by limiting the number of people who could carry the truckers' message and, therefore, the audience they could reach. The Court said the restrictions also made it less likely the truckers could gather enough signatures to place the deregulation issue on the ballot. Furthermore, it did not matter to the Court that the truckers might deliver their message to the public through other channels. "Colorado's prohibition of paid circulators," Stevens wrote, "restricts access to the most effective, fundamental, and perhaps economical avenue of political discourse, direct one-on-one communication."

The Court rejected Colorado's argument that paid solicitors might jeopardize the integrity of the initiative process by accepting false signatures. The Court saw no reason why paid professionals seeking signatures should be any more willing than unpaid volunteers to face criminal prosecution for collecting false signatures.

ELECTIONS

Permitted Corporate and Union Election Communications (p. 272)

In 1989, the United States District Court for the District of Columbia ruled that the National Organization of Women could send membership solicitation letters critical of Republicans without violating the ban on corporate election expenditures.[2] The letters, sent to the public during the election campaigns of 1984, urged political action to counter the policies of Republicans. Some politicians named in the letters were running for re-election.

The district court said the letters naturally invoked the names of politicians because the letters discussed public issues. But the court said the membership solicitation letters did not violate the election laws because they did not "expressly advocate" the election or

---

[2]Fed. Election Comm'n v. Nat'l Org. for Women, 2 Fed. Election Camp. Fin. Guide (CCH) para. 9274 (May 11, 1989).

defeat of the named candidates. The letters' call for political action could have invited demonstrations, lobbying, letter writing, and other forms of political advocacy besides voting against Republican candidates, the court said.

Political Action Committees

Solicitation of Funds (pp. 275-276) The U.S. Court of Appeals for the District of Columbia Circuit ruled in 1988 that independent committees may use a candidate's name in fund-raising materials and still remain "independent" of the candidate.[3] The court said a committee remains independent while using a candidate's name as long as the candidate's name is not part of the official name of the committee.

Restrictions on Individuals and Groups in Elections

Disclosure (pp. 280-281)

The Supreme Court refused to review an appeals court ruling requiring disclosure of the sponsor of a campaign ad. A federal appeals court ruled that the sponsor of an ad may have to be disclosed even if the ad does not expressly ask citizens to vote for the candidate. In *Federal Election Commission v. Furgatch*,[4] the Ninth Circuit Court of Appeals ruled that Harvey Furgatch's anti-Carter advertisements in 1980 violated the election disclosure law because they neither named Furgatch as the sponsor nor carried a disclaimer that the ads were not authorized by the candidate. The ad said: "The President of the United States continues degrading the electoral process" and "His meanness of spirit is divisive."

Furgatch argued disclosure of the sponsor of the ads was not required because the ads did not "expressly advocate" the election or defeat of President Carter. But the Ninth Circuit said the ad, read as a whole, is "susceptible of no other reasonable interpretation but as an exortation to vote for or against a specific candidate."

LOBBYING: THE RIGHT TO PETITION

Foreign Agents

Propaganda (pp. 284-285)

In May 1988, the U.S. Court of Appeals for the Ninth Circuit declared unconstitutional the U.S. Information Agency's regulations for certifying American films for export as "educational, scientific and cultural."[5] Films that are designated educational, scientific, or cultural may be imported into other countries duty-free under provisions of the "Beirut

---

[3]Common Cause v. Fed. Election Comm'n, 842 F.2d 436 (D.C. Cir. 1988).

[4]807 F.2d 857 (1987), *cert. denied*, 108 S. Ct. 151 (1987).

[5]Bullfrog Films Inc. v. Wick, 56 U.S.L.W. 2670 (May 31, 1988).

Agreement." The 72 countries that signed the Beirut Agreement hoped to encourage production and distribution of non-commercial educational films by allowing them to be sold internationally without duties. Under the agreement, each country exporting films determines the criteria for designating films educational, scientific, or cultural.

The U.S. Information Agency denied the educational designation to any films that "by special pleading attempt generally to influence opinion, conviction or policy" or "to espouse a cause." The agency's regulations also barred the educational label for films that appeared "to attack or discredit economic, religious, or political views or practices." Materials that engaged in special pleading or attacked political views could be labeled "propaganda."

The Ninth Circuit said the regulations were unconstitutional because they limited expression of opinion on issues of public controversy protected by the First Amendment. The court also said the regulations were unconstitutionally vague. The court said an ordinary person would be hard pressed to define "special pleading" or "to espouse a cause" in the regulations.

COMMUNICATION BETWEEN LABOR AND MANAGEMENT (pp. 287-289)

The Supreme Court ruled that federal labor law permits a union to distribute handbills urging the public not to patronize a shopping mall. In *DeBartolo Corp. v. Florida Gulf Coast Building and Construction Trades Council*,[6] the Court ruled 6-2 that peaceful distribution of handbills is not illegally coercive even if the purpose of the handbills is to pressure merchants to oppose construction by non-union workers. The Court noted that the union did not engage in coercive picketing or patrolling. The union was only trying to persuade customers not to shop in the mall. Handbills, unlike coercive picketing, the Court said, depend for their effectiveness entirely on the persuasive force of the ideas they convey.

Because the Court decided the case by interpreting the labor statute, the Court did not make a First Amendment ruling. But the Court noted that a union handbill revealing a labor dispute and urging shoppers to buy elsewhere is political speech protected by the First Amendment.

SECURITIES TRANSACTIONS

Fraud (p. 299)

In an effort to deter and punish insider trading, Congress in 1988 passed legislation that increases penalties, extends liability, and encourages revelation of insider trading. The

---

[6]108 S. Ct. 1392 (1988).

Insider Trading and Securities Fraud Enforcement Act of 1988 was passed in an attempt to curb the increasing number of Wall Street scandals.[7] Under the new law, not only are illegal traders and tippers liable, but also those brokers, investment advisers, and other supervisors who fail to take appropriate steps to prevent illegal trading. The act also increases criminal penalties and allows the Securities and Exchange Commission to pay persons who provide information concerning insider trading.

Materially Deceptive Facts

Omissions (pp. 300-302) The Supreme Court agreed with the Sixth Circuit Court of Appeals in *Basic, Inc. v. Levinson* [8] (pp. 301-302) that information about corporate mergers may be "material" before an agreement-in-principle is reached between negotiating corporations. Basic, Inc., had argued that it was not fraudulent for the company to falsely deny merger negotiations before an agreement had been struck. The company said such early negotiations are not material and therefore would not affect an investor's decision to buy or sell.

The Court rejected Basic's argument that investors would be overwhelmed by trivial details if companies had to reveal merger information before the negotiating companies had reached an agreement. Basic's desire to protect investors from "trivia" is a paternalistic attitude that "assumes that investors are nitwits," the Court said.

The Court did not define the exact point at which merger information becomes material. That point depends on the facts of each case. A company determines materiality of an omitted fact or misleading corporate statement, the Court said, by weighing the probability of a merger and the magnitude of the transaction to the company. Probability is to be determined by an examination of board resolutions, instructions to investment bankers, the number of negotiations, and other evidence of interest in the merger among corporate executives. The magnitude of the merger depends on the size of the corporations involved and the potential payments above market value of the company.

Under the Court's probability/magnitude test, merger negotiations must be disclosed if the new company resulting from the merger would dramatically alter the company, even if the odds of a merger are remote. Similarly, negotiations must be revealed if they have reached an advanced state, even if the merger will not greatly affect the structure of the company.

Even after the *Basic* ruling, companies may still remain silent about on-going merger negotiations. How much to reveal becomes a problem only if the company chooses to speak. But silence may be difficult to maintain when a company is pressed by securities analysts and the media to explain volatility in a company's stock. Nevertheless, companies may find it necessary to stonewall the media, as one legal expert suggests, by

---

[7]Pub. L. 100-704, 102 Stat. 4677 (Nov. 199, 1988). *See also*, H. Rpt. No. 100-910, 100th Cong., 2d sess., *reprinted in* 1988 *U.S. Code Cong. & Ad. News* 6043.

[8]108 S. Ct. 978 (1988).

saying "no comment."[9] Alternatives to silence may be unacceptable to a company. If a company reveals the negotiations, a merger may fall through; if a company provides incomplete or misleading public statements, it commits fraud.

While the Court said that pre-agreement merger information may be material, the Court did not rule whether Basic's denial of merger negotiations was materially misleading. The Court remanded the case for a determination of whether Basic's denial of merger negotiations was material as measured by the Court's probability/magnitude standard.

Failure to Disclose Payment for Publicity (p. 303) In 1989, the Supreme Court refused to review a federal appeals court ruling that kept alive a fraud case against *Stock Market Magazine.* The Securities and Exchange Commission charged the magazine with fraud for failing to reveal advertising and reprints sold to companies featured in the publication.[10] The case was remanded to the district court to determine whether the magazine, which offers financial news to some 12,000 subscribers, was publishing the articles in exchange for corporate purchases of advertising and reprints. If so, the magazine could be required to disclose this "consideration." The magazine contended there was no *quid pro quo* that needed to be revealed under the securities laws.

The U.S. Court of Appeals for the District of Columbia told the district court that the fraud inquiry could not include examination of the origin of articles published in the magazine. The Securities and Exchange Commission had argued that *Stock Market Magazine* should be required to reveal not only that it sold advertising and reprints, but also that featured companies sometimes wrote the articles, paid public relations firms to write them, or paid editors of the *Stock Market Magazine* itself to write them. The SEC charged that the free articles, which *Stock Market Magazine* published "substantially" as received, also constituted "consideration" that must be disclosed under securities law.

The appeals court said the First Amendment prohibits inquiry into who pays a writer or how much of an outside article is published. Such inquiry, the court said, would impermissibly interfere with editorial judgments about constitutionally protected content. The First Amendment protects the publisher's right to determine who writes and edits published material, the court said. Content is protected if the writer is paid by a publisher, a public relations firm, or a featured company. Disclosure might be required, the court said, if a magazine received payments or sold advertising and reprints as a condition for publishing an article, but requiring disclosure of who wrote certain parts of a business article is unconstitutional.

In another case, the publisher of *Stockbroker Special Situations Newsletter* pleaded no contest in 1989 to charges that he failed to disclose cash and stock received to publish

---

9"Post-Winans Insider Trading Law Debated by Lawyer's at ALI-ABA Seminar," 20 *Sec. Reg. & L. Rep.* (BNA) 329, 330 (March 4, 1988).

10SEC v. Wall St. Publishing Inst., 851 F.2d 365 (D.D. Cir. 1988), *cert. denied*, 57 U.S.L.W. 3588 (March 7, 1989).

favorable stories about eight stocks.[11] The SEC claimed the newsletter publisher touted the stocks in return for $17,000 in payments from each of seven companies and $22,000 in stock from another.

Duty to Disclose

Financial Journalists and Market Insiders (pp. 309-311) The Supreme Court unanimously affirmed the conviction of R. Foster Winans for wire and mail fraud and, in a 4-4 vote, affirmed the former *Wall Street Journal* employee's conviction for securities fraud.[12] The Court ruled that Winans violated the wire and mail fraud statutes by misappropriating confidential information belonging to his employer and using it for his own gain in violation of the *Wall Street Journal's* conflict of interest policy.

In an opinion written by Justice White, the Court said the unpublished news Winans provided to his broker for stock purchases was confidential property belonging to Winans' employer, the *Wall Street Journal.* The Court said Winans fraudulently misappropriated this property when he gave it to the broker, Peter Brant, for illegal trading. The Court said the mail and wire statutes were violated because Winans' fraudulent scheme depended on publication of the *Journal*; publication requires use of telephone wires and the mail.

Four justices voted to affirm Winans' conviction for securities fraud and four voted against it. The split vote affirmed the conviction in the second circuit. None of the justices explained his or her vote in an opinion, but they apparently split on whether Winans' conduct was "in connection with" securities sales as required by the securities laws (p. 303). Conduct is "in connection with" the purchase or sale of securities when it involves material inside information and the purchasers or sellers of stock.

All of the justices presumably found Winans' misappropriation fraudulent under the securities statutes, just as they did under the wire and mail fraud statutes. Therefore, the justices apparently disagreed whether Winans should be liable under the securities laws because the case did not involve inside corporate information. The information Winans misappropriated circulated publicly even before it was published in the *Wall Street Journal.* Also raising a question whether Winans' fraud was "in connection with" securities transactions is the fact that the *Wall Street Journal* was not a purchaser or seller of stocks.

In December 1988, a former *Business Week* news broadcaster pleaded guilty to mail fraud for trading on information from the magazine's "Inside Wall Street" column. The journalist, S. G. "Rudy" Ruderman, made about $15,000 over 2 1/2 years trading on information from *Business Week* before the magazine was published.[13]

---

[11]"Publisher Settles SEC Complaint," *News Media Update,* Oct. 29, 1988, at 3.

[12]Carpenter v. U.S., 108 S. Ct. 3316 (1987).

[13]"Ruderman Pleads Guilty to Charges of Mail Fraud," *Wall Street Journal,* Dec. 9, 1988, at B6.

7
ADVERTISING

The 100th Congress passed several laws affecting advertising. A major revision of trademark law allows companies to sue more easily over false claims in competitors' ads. Other legislation permits advertising of lotteries by non-profit groups and dissemination of information about bingo on Indian reservations.

As the *Update* went to press, the Federal Trade Commission was still deciding whether an editorial advertisement by the R.J. Reynolds Tobacco Company is fully protected political speech, or is less-protected commercial speech. In the meantime, the Supreme Court amended the four-part test for commercial speech to permit slightly broader regulation. The Court also ruled that attorneys may send letters soliciting business to people facing legal problems.

In important negligence decisions during the last two years, the Fifth Circuit reversed a $9.4 million verdict against the publisher of an advertisement that led to an assassination. Another federal court ruled that a trial should be held to determine whether a public relations firm is liable for a costly error in a commercial report.

THE FIRST AMENDMENT AND ADVERTISING (pp. 316-329)

In 1989, the Supreme Court ruled that lower courts should decide whether regulations barring "private commercial enterprises" on university property violate the First Amendment rights of students at the State University of New York at Cortland. Students challenged the regulations on grounds they unconstitutionally restrict both commercial and noncommercial speech. The students said the regulations were used to bar them from hosting "Tupperware parties" in their dorm rooms where they would not only discuss silverware and china, but also noncommercial subjects such as financial responsibility and efficient homemaking. The Court ruled 6-3 in *Board of Trustees of the State University of New York v. Fox* that a lower court should decide whether the regulation unconstitutionally restricted the students' commercial and noncommercial speech.[1]

Writing for the majority, Justice Scalia broadened the Court's four-part test for determining the constitutionality of regulations on commercial speech. Scalia said that restrictions on commercial speech may be constitutional even if they are not the "least restrictive" possible. Some lower courts thought the Supreme Court had earlier required the least restrictive regulations when the Court said that regulations on commercial speech must be no broader than necessary to advance government interests. In *Fox*, the Court said regulations on commercial speech must be "narrowly tailored" to meet legislative purposes, but they do not have to be the "least restrictive." Scalia said there should be a reasonable "fit" between legislative interests and the regulations employed to achieve them.

The three dissenters in *Fox* would have declared the state university regulations unconstitutionally overbroad. A prohibition on "private commercial enterprises," the dissenters said, unconstitutionally bars protected dorm-room conversations between students and doctors, lawyers, tutors, speech therapists, and other paid counsellors.

In 1988, the Supreme Court extended the right of attorneys to advertise by ruling that they may mail solicitations directly to people known to face legal problems (p. 319). In *Shapero v. Kentucky Bar Association*, the Court ruled that attorney Richard D. Shapero could send letters offering help to homeowners facing foreclosure.[2] "Call NOW," the letter urged. "It may surprise you what I may be able to do for you."

In *Shapero*, the Court struck down a Kentucky Supreme Court rule prohibiting attorneys from mailing advertisements to potential clients who, because of a specific event, might need legal services. The rule was supposed to prevent attorneys from taking advantage of people when their judgment might be impaired by misfortune. The state argued that an attorney's letter, like an in-person solicitation, exerts undue influence on a vulnerable person. In 1978, the Supreme Court ruled that lawyers' in-person solicitations may be barred because they pose a threat of undue influence (p. 324).

In *Shapero*, the Court ruled 6-3 that an attorney's mailing does not pose the same risk of undue influence as an in-person solicitation. A client receiving a letter, unlike a client talking to an attorney, can put the communication in a drawer for later consideration. A written communication, even to a distraught person, the Court said, does not coerce or invade privacy the way that a personal solicitation might.

[1]57 U.S.L.W. 5015 (June 29, 1989).

[2]108 S. Ct. 1916 (1988). The Court also refused to review a lower court decision involving a California bar regulation that assumes testimonial advertisements by attorneys are misleading. The Supreme Court dismissed the case for want of a properly presented federal question. Oring v. State Bar of California, 109 S. Ct. 1562 (1989).

The Court said in *Shapero* that a state may bar misleading attorneys' letters but can not prohibit letters entirely. The Court suggested that misleading letters might include those that unduly emphasize trivial or uninformative facts or offer exaggerated assurances of client satisfaction. After striking down the Kentucky rule banning letters, the Court sent the case back to the lower court to determine whether Richard Shapero's letter was deceptive.

In 1989, the Supreme Court dismissed an appeal from Minnesota challenging the federal restrictions on lottery advertising.[3] The Court said a new federal lottery law, discussed later in the chapter, made it unnecessary to decide the Minnesota questions.

Commercial Speech Eligible for Constitutional Consideration

Commercial Speech (pp. 321-322)

In 1989, a federal appeals court refused to review a case in which the Federal Trade Commission is deciding whether a cigarette company's editorial advertisement is commercial speech or political speech. The Federal Appeals Court for the District of Columbia said it would not review the R.J. Reynolds advertisement until the Federal Trade Commission decides to what degree the advertisement, "Of Cigarettes and Science," may be protected by the First Amendment (see next page for the ad).

In 1988, the Federal Trade Commission told an administrative law judge in the agency to consider whether the content of the ad and R.J. Reynolds's commercial motives make the editorial ad commercial speech.[4] The commission, in a 4-1 decision, noted that the paid ad, like other ads ruled to be commercial speech, referred to a specific product--cigarettes--and discussed an important attribute of the product--scientists' charges of a link between smoking and heart disease. The administrative law judge had earlier dismissed the complaint against the tobacco company on grounds that the ad is constitutionally protected political opinion.

In a case involving a public relations firm, the Federal District Court for the District of Columbia ruled that a consultant's economic report is commercial speech.[5] The court ruled that a $75,000 report prepared by Booz-Allen & Hamilton for the Georgia Ports Authority was commercial speech, rather than political speech, because Booz-Allen prepared "objective factual data" on behalf of "a seller embarking on a marketing campaign."

The "objective facts" in the report were statements based on noncommercial data, maps, and charts, which compared the ports of Savannah, Georgia, and Charleston, South Carolina. The "seller" mentioned by the court was the Georgia Ports Authority, which commissioned the 80-page report as part of a campaign to win customers for the

---

[3]Frank v. Minnesota Newspaper Ass'n, Inc., 109 S. Ct. 1734.

[4]R.J. Reynolds Tobacco Co., 3 *Trade Reg. Rep.* (CCH) para. 22, 522 (June 2, 1988).

[5]South Carolina State Ports Authority v. Booz-Allen & Hamilton, Inc., 676 F. Supp. 346, 14 Med. L. Rptr. 2132 (D.C.D.C. 1987).

Of cigarettes and science.

This is the way science is supposed to work.

A scientist observes a certain set of facts. To explain these facts, the scientist comes up with a theory.

Then, to check the validity of the theory, the scientist performs an experiment. If the experiment yields positive results, and is duplicated by other scientists, then the theory is supported. If the experiment produces negative results, the theory is re-examined, modified or discarded.

But, to a scientist, both positive and negative results should be important. Because both produce valuable learning.

Now let's talk about cigarettes.

You probably know about research that links smoking to certain diseases. Coronary heart disease is one of them.

Much of this evidence consists of studies that show a statistical association between smoking and the disease.

But statistics themselves cannot explain *why* smoking and heart disease are associated. Thus, scientists have developed a theory: that heart disease is *caused* by smoking. Then they performed various experiments to check this theory.

We would like to tell you about one of the most important of these experiments.

A little-known study

It was called the Multiple Risk Factor Intervention Trial (MR FIT).

In the words of the *Wall Street Journal,* it was "one of the largest medical experiments ever attempted." Funded by the Federal government, it cost $115,000,000 and took 10 years, ending in 1982.

The subjects were over 12,000 men who were thought to have a high risk of heart disease because of three risk factors

that are statistically associated with this disease: smoking, high blood pressure and high cholesterol levels.

Half of the men received no special medical intervention. The other half received medical treatment that consistently reduced all three risk factors, compared with the first group.

It was assumed that the group with lower risk factors would, over time, suffer significantly fewer deaths from heart disease than the higher risk factor group.

But that is not the way it turned out.

After 10 years, there was no statistically significant difference between the two groups in the number of heart disease deaths.

The theory persists

We at R.J. Reynolds do not claim this study proves that smoking doesn't cause heart disease. But we do wish to make a point.

Despite the results of MR FIT and other experiments like it, many scientists have not abandoned or modified their original theory, or re-examined its assumptions.

They continue to believe these factors cause heart disease. But it is important to label their belief accurately. It is an opinion. A judgment. But *not* scientific fact.

We believe in science. That is why we continue to provide funding for independent research into smoking and health.

But we do not believe there should be one set of scientific principles for the whole world, and a different set for experiments involving cigarettes. Science is science. Proof is proof. That is why the controversy over smoking and health remains an open one.

R.J. Reynolds Tobacco Company

(Reproduced with the permission of R.J. Reynolds Tobacco Co.)

Savannah port. In a negligence suit over the accuracy of the report, the federal court said Booz-Allen, like a commercial advertiser, was "in a position to verify the accuracy of its factual representations; indeed, that appeared to be one of its primary tasks." The negligence suit is discussed shortly.

UNFAIR AND DECEPTIVE ADVERTISING

Deception

Tendency to Deceive

Comparative Advertisements (pp. 338-340) Congress in 1988 revamped the Lanham Trademark Act (p. 339) to allow a company to sue if advertisers or public relations firms misrepresent their own or a competitor's products or services. Under the Lanham Act of 1946, companies could sue advertisers who misrepresented their own products or services, but not advertisers who misrepresented a competitor's products or services. The Trademark Law Revision Act of 1988 amended section 43(a) to allow a company to sue if it thinks it will be hurt by another's use of a false or misleading fact "in commercial advertising or promotion." A misleading fact "misrepresents the nature, characteristics, qualities, or geographic origin of his or her or another person's goods, services, or commercial activities."[6]

The new law leaves the courts to determine what constitutes a "fact" and "commercial advertising and promotion." The courts will also decide whether significant omissions in ads and promotions are deceptive under section 43(a).[7] Section 43(a) does not allow suits over false statements in news stories or political advertisements.

Lotteries (pp. 340-342) In November 1988, President Reagan signed into law a bill permitting advertising of lotteries. The old law permitted mail and broadcast advertising of official state lotteries in the state that runs them and in adjacent states. The new law, the Charity Games Advertising Clarification Act of 1988, permits advertising of all official state lotteries in any state that operates one.[8] The new law also permits print or broadcast advertising and publication of prize lists of lotteries conducted by non-profit organizations. Furthermore, commercial companies may advertise an occasional promotional lottery if it is not related to the company's usual business.

Under the new law, mail and broadcast advertising for lotteries may be barred for any game that is illegal under state law. The Charity Games Act does not go into effect until May 1990, giving states 18 months to revise their lottery laws.

---

[6]Pub. L. 100-667, sec. 132, *amending* sec. 43(a), 15 U.S.C. 1125(a).

[7]*See*, S. Rep. No. 100-515, 100th Cong., 2d sess. 41- 42, *reprinted in* 1988 U.S. Code Cong. & Ad. News 5603-04.

[8]Pub. L. 100-625, 102 Stat. 3205 (Nov. 7, 1988).

In other gambling legislation, Congress permitted broadcast and publication about bingo and similar games conducted on Indian reservations. Under provisions of the Indian Gaming Regulatory Act, dissemination of information about gaming on Indian reservations is permitted as long as the games are legal under state law.[9]

Negligence (New section to be inserted on p. 343)

In August 1989, the U.S. Court of Appeals for the Fifth Circuit overturned a $9.4 million judgment against *Soldier of Fortune* magazine for negligently publishing an advertisement that led to an assassination.[10] The appeals court said the district court was wrong to rule that the magazine had a duty not to print a classified ad for "High Risk Assignments" that resulted in a contract killing. Consistent with many other courts, the Fifth Circuit said the burden on publishers would be too great if they had to reject all ads that might result in harm to readers.

Publishers, like anyone else, are negligent if they injure someone by failing to act reasonably when they have a duty to others. In determining negligence, courts weigh the risk of harm against the burden of preventing that harm. In *Soldier of Fortune*, the Fifth Circuit concluded that the burden on publishers of rejecting all ads that might result in harm was too great. Indeed, the court said it would be virtually impossible for a publisher to foresee which ads might prevent a grave danger.

The *Soldier of Fortune* case arose from a suit by the mother and son of a Sandra Black who was assassinated by a man named John Wayne Hearn. Hearn ran an advertisement in *Soldier of Fortune* that said: "EX-MARINES. -- '67-69 'Nam vets . . . weapons specialist -- jungle warfare, pilot . . . high risk assignments U.S. or overseas." Black's husband hired Hearn to murder his wife.

Black's mother and son convinced a jury that *Soldier of Fortune* was negligent because the magazine should have known that a person placing an advertisement with terms such as "high risk assignments" was soliciting illegal activity. "High risk assignments," the relatives said, is a term commonly used to advertise contract killing. Several other ads in the magazine had also been linked to violent crimes. The jurors awarded Black's son and mother actual damages of more than $1.9 million and punitive damages of $7.5 million.

The Fifth Circuit, however, ruled that the district court imposed too high a standard of conduct on *Soldier of Fortune*. The Fifth Circuit agreed that *Soldier of Fortune* owed a duty of reasonable care to protect the public from such serious crimes as murder, but the court said the magazine had not violated that duty. Given the ambiguous nature of Hearn's ad and the pervasiveness of advertising in American society, the court said, one could not expect a publisher to foresee that the advertisement would lead to a murder.

---

[9]Pub. L. 100-497, 102 Stat. 2467 (1988).

[10]Eimann v. Soldier of Fortune, 1989 WL 85101 (Aug. 17, 1989).

The ad did not directly recruit for illegal assignments. Indeed, an advertisement for "high risk assignments" could have sought bodyguards, as Hearn claimed, not assassins, the court said. Furthermore, the link between other ads in the magazine and crime would not necessarily mean that Hearn was seeking criminal activity. Even had the publisher of *Soldier of Fortune* checked Hearn's background before running the advertisement, he would have found no criminal record. Such ambiguity, the court said "provides no reliable method for gauging the likelihood that a particular ad will foster illegal activity." Publishers cannot be held liable for negligence in such ambiguous circumstances, the court said.

Soldier of Fortune is consistent with cases in which publishers have not been held liable for unintentional, non-libelous, errors in news or advertisements, even if those errors cause harm.[11] Nevertheless, in a public relations case, a federal court has held that a consulting firm may be liable for negligently publishing misleading commercial information that causes economic harm. The U.S. District Court for the District of Columbia denied summary judgment for Booz-Allen & Hamilton, Inc., in a negligence suit over the firm's allegedly misleading report.[12] The South Carolina State Ports Authority charged that the $75,000 report commissioned by the Georgia Ports Authority contained false information about the depth and convenience of the port at Charleston. The errors, South Carolina said, hurt the state in its commercial competition with Georgia.

SELF-REGULATION (pp. 355-359)

With the end of the Reagan Administration, the period of deregulation championed by conservatives waned. "The era of deregulation is coming to an end, and we are going to see increasing pressure in Congress and in the states to regulate advertising and to tax advertising," said Howard Bell, president of the American Advertising Federation.[13]

Indeed, pressures for regulation have increased. State attorneys general aggressively try to bar deceptive advertising when they think federal regulation is lax. Twenty-five state attorneys general filed a suit against the Department of Transportation over an order permitting airlines to exclude certain fees from advertised air fares. The National Association of Attorneys General argues that airlines mislead when they omit fees from

---

11*E.g.*, First Equity Corp. of Florida v. Standard & Poor's Corp., 670 F. Supp. 115, 14 Med. L. Rptr. 1945, (S.D.N.Y. 1987), *aff'd*, 869 F. 2d 175, 16 Med. L. Rptr. 1282 (2d Cir. 1989) (error in bond report); Pittman v. Dow Jones, 662 F. Supp. 921, 14 Med. L. Rptr. 1284 (E.D. La. 1987), *aff'd.*, 834 F.2d 1171, 14 Med. L. Rptr. 2384 (5th Cir. 1987) (misleading ad for investment); Jaillet v. Cashman, 115 Misc. 383, 189 N.Y.S. 743 (Sup. Ct. 1921), *aff'd mem.*, 202 A.D. 805, 194 N.Y.S. 947 (1922), *aff'd mem.*, 235 N.Y. 511, 139 N.E. 714 (1923) (error in stock reports); Daniel v. Dow Jones & Co., 520 N.Y.S. 2d 334, 14 Med. L. Rptr. 1995 (N.Y. City Civ. Ct. 1987) (error in computerized news service).

12South Carolina State Ports Authority v. Booz-Allen & Hamilton, Inc., 676 F. Supp. 346, 14 Med. L. Rptr. 2132 (D.C.D.C. 1987).

13"AAF hears warnings of turning tide," *Broadcasting*, March 21, 1988, at 46.

advertised ticket fares. The National Association of Attorneys General has also investigated car rental advertising and health claims in food advertisements and labels.

Federal and state lawmakers are also introducing bills to regulate the sale of
cigarettes, ban tobacco advertisements, and require package warnings such as the
Surgeon General's finding that nicotine is addictive. Bills to ban corporate tax
deductions for tobacco advertising have also been introduced.

Some advertisers have promoted self-regulation to stave off a resurgence of
government regulation. The Direct Mail Board of Review, Inc., a group formed to help
regulate direct mail advertising, has issued a new Code of Business Ethics. The
American Telemarketing Association has also adopted "Telemarketing Standards and
Ethics Guidelines."

To calm would-be government regulators, advertising associations have urged
television networks not to curtail their scrutiny of broadcast commercials. In letters to
the networks, the president of the American Association of Advertising Agencies said
network attempts to save money by cutting the staff members who review commercials
"invite government regulation to fill the void."[14] Networks say staff reductions will not
diminish broadcasters' scrutiny of advertisements for deception.

[14]Gordon, "Networks hit for ad clearance cuts," *Advertising Age*, Sept. 12, 1988, at 6.

8
PORNOGRAPHY

The U.S. Supreme Court during the last two years ruled unconstitutional an Indiana statute permitting the government to seize pornographic materials before they have been ruled obscene. The Court also vacated a Massachusetts Supreme Court decision striking down a statute punishing photography of nude children. In a third decision, the Court ruled that telephone pornography is constitutionally protected (see Chapter 12). In mid-1989, a federal statute to protect children from obscenity took effect.

INTRODUCTION

Due Process and Prior Restraints (p. 363)

In *Fort Wayne Books Inc. v. Indiana*, the U.S. Supreme Court ruled in 1989 that government agents may not seize sexual materials before a judge has determined at a hearing they are obscene.[1] The U.S. Supreme Court overturned a decision of the Supreme Court of Indiana holding that all sexual materials in an adult bookstore might be removed before trial if officials had reason to believe that obscenity was being circulated. The U.S. Supreme Court said the risk of prior restraint on constitutionally protected expression is too high if sexual materials may be seized before they are found to be obscene. The Court said officials may seize a single copy of a book or film as evidence, but they may not take all materials from an adult bookstore before an obscenity determination is made.

---

[1] 16 Med. L. Rptr. 1337 (1989).

In a child pornography case, the Supreme Court vacated and remanded a Massachusetts decision declaring a state pornography statute unconstitutionally overbroad.[2] The Massachusetts statute made it a crime to film, photograph or exhibit nude children under 18 or to have children participate in sexual conduct. Violators were subject to prison terms of 10-20 years and fines of up to $50,000. A Massachusetts resident, Douglas Oakes, was convicted under the law and sentenced to 10 years in prison for taking photographs of his physically mature 14-year-old stepdaughter wearing only bikini pants and a scarf. Officials learned of the photos from Oakes' wife.

The Supreme Judicial Court of Massachusetts had ruled 4-3 the statute was unconstitutionally overbroad because it made a crime out of such innocent behavior as photographing a nude baby "running on a beach."[3] The Massachusetts court, which overturned Oakes' conviction, said "artists who painted some of the world's greatest paintings" would have been criminals under the statute. Because the Massachusetts court ruled the statute might be unconstitutional in some circumstances, it never considered whether it was unconstitutional as applied to Douglas Oakes' pictures.

The U.S. Supreme Court did not decide whether the Massachusetts statute was too broad. After Oakes was convicted, the Massachusetts legislature narrowed the statute so that parents taking innocent photos of nude children would not be prosecuted. After the law was amended, it was a crime in Massachusetts to film, photograph, or exhibit a nude minor only if done with a "lascivious intent." With the law modified, the Supreme Court said the overbreadth issue was moot. But the Court did send the case back to Massachusetts for determination of whether Oakes' conviction was constitutional.

To combat child pornography, Congress passed legislation in 1988 making it a crime to sell minors for sexually explicit conduct. The Child Protection and Obscenity Enforcement Act of 1988, which went into effect in August 1989, also requires publishers, printers, photographers, and filmmakers to be able to show that persons depicted in sexual activity are at least 18 years old.[4] Several publishing groups challenged the constitutionality of the record-keeping requirements in the act, requirements that the publishers say are unconstitutionally burdensome.[5]

REGULATING NONOBSCENE SEXUAL EXPRESSION

Display Laws (p. 382)

In a case remanded by the U.S. Supreme Court, the Virginia Supreme Court held that 16 books by James Joyce, John Updike, Judy Blume, and other authors would not be banned

---

[2]Massachusetts v. Oakes, 57 U.S.L.W. 4787 (1989).

[3]Massachusetts v. Oakes, 518 N.E.2d 836 (1987).

[4]Pub. L. 100-690, 102 Stat. 4485 (1988).

[5]"New Pornography Curb Challenged," *New York Times*, March 13, 1989, at 8.

under a state statute protecting minors from "harmful" material (p. 383).[6] Booksellers feared that the books, several of which have considerable literary merit, could be barred under the statute protecting minors from sexually explicit books and films. In an interpretive decision requested by the U.S. Supreme Court,[7] the Virginia court ruled that none of the 16 books would be banned under the statute that bars display of harmful materials in such a way that juveniles might "examine and peruse" them.

The Virginia court also ruled that store owners do not have to bar display of harmful materials entirely to keep juveniles from examining them. It is sufficient, the Virginia court said, for booksellers to keep sexually explicit materials in sight so that juveniles may be halted if they attempt to peruse them.

---

[6]Virginia v. American Booksellers Ass'n, 15 Med. L. Rptr. 2078 (Va. 1988).

[7]Virginia v. American Booksellers Ass'n, 108 S. Ct. 636 (1988).

9
THE MEDIA AND THE JUDICIARY

In the spring of 1988, the U.S. Supreme Court decided *U.S. v. Providence Journal* on procedural grounds rather than deciding whether a newspaper has a right to ignore an unconstitutional prior restraint order.

In the last few years, several states have adopted rules allowing cameras in court. Two states have denied access to cameras.

Several courts have recognized a right of public access to juvenile proceedings, and to both civil and criminal court records, sometimes even when those records were not used in evidence in a trial. However, courts continue to find that neither the First Amendment nor the common law guarantee access to all judicial records and proceedings.

CONTEMPT POWER

Disobeying a Court Order (pp. 402-404)

In May 1988, the U.S. Supreme Court dismissed a case that might have resolved confusion over whether a newspaper can ignore, without penalty, an apparently unconstitutional prior restraint on publication (pp. 402-404). Because the Supreme Court dismissed *U.S. v. Providence Journal* on procedural grounds, it did not decide whether a newspaper has a First Amendment right to disobey a judge's order prohibiting publication.[1]

The Supreme Court dismissed a writ of *certiorari* it had originally granted on an appeal of a decision by the U.S. Court of Appeals for the First Circuit. The First Circuit

---

[1] 108 S. Ct. 1502, 15 Med. L. Rptr. 1241 (1988).

had overturned a contempt conviction handed down by a federal district court judge against the *Providence Journal* and its editor Charles Hauser (p. 403).[2] Because the Supreme Court dismissed the writ of *certiorari*, the First Circuit's ruling in favor of the newspaper stands.

The *Providence Journal*, contrary to a judicial order, printed information it obtained from the FBI about Raymond L. S. Patriarca, a reputed crime boss in New England. The FBI had released the results of an illegal wiretap after Patriarca died in 1985. However, Patriarca's son obtained a court order barring publication in the *Journal* on the grounds that his own right of privacy would be violated. The *Journal* was cited for contempt of court in November 1986 when it printed a story based on the FBI file in violation of the court order.

A three-judge panel of the First Circuit reversed the contempt order a month later. The panel said the order was a "transparently invalid" infringement of the First Amendment because the federal district judge had failed to meet the heavy burden of proof required by the U.S. Supreme Court before prior restraints can be imposed (pp. 403-404). In May 1987, the First Circuit, after rehearing the case *en banc*, affirmed the panel's opinion but attached a modification. The full court said that editors in the future must make a "good faith effort" to appeal a prior restraint order that appears to be "transparently unconstitutional." When editors are ordered not to print a story, the court said, they may publish and still challenge the constitutionality of an order only "if timely access to the appellate court is not available or if [a] timely decision is not forthcoming."[3]

The First Circuit said it would have been "unfair" to apply its new requirement to the *Providence Journal* after the fact. Further, the court said, it was not sure whether "timely emergency relief" was available to the *Journal*.

Less than a year later, the Supreme Court ruled 7-1 that the case against the *Journal* had to be dismissed because the prosecutor who argued it before the Court did so without the approval of former U.S. Solicitor General Charles Fried. A federal statute requires the solicitor general to authorize all petitions of *certiorari* filed with the Supreme Court on behalf of the federal government. The prosecutor who took the case to the Supreme Court had been appointed by the federal district judge issuing the contempt order. Solicitor General Fried refused to give the prosecutor the authority to file for a writ of *certiorari*.

CONTROLLING CONDUCT IN COURT

Cameras Move into Courtrooms (pp. 407-411)

Since the summer of 1987, several states have adopted temporary or permanent rules allowing cameras in courtrooms, pushing to 45 the number of states allowing audio-

---

[2]*In re* Providence Journal, 13 Med. L. Rptr. 1945 (1st Cir. 1987).

[3]*In re* Providence Journal, 820 F.2d 1354, 14 Med. L. Rptr. 1029 (1st Cir. 1987).

visual coverage of court proceedings. However, the Indiana and South Carolina supreme courts decided not to permit cameras into courts in those states.

Since *The Law of Public Communication* was published, six states--Hawaii, Kansas, Michigan, North Dakota, Oregon, and Rhode Island--have permitted journalists to use cameras in all courts.[4] Experiments with cameras in trial courts have been extended in New York[5] and reinstated in Minnesota.[6] Both states already allowed cameras in appellate courts.

In contrast, the South Carolina Supreme Court in 1988 rejected a proposal to experiment with cameras and tape recorders in the state's circuit courts. The Indiana Supreme Court denied in 1987 a petition to allow cameras in courtrooms. The only other states that still ban cameras from courtrooms are Missouri, Mississippi, and South Dakota.

Media cameras are also still banned in the District of Columbia and in federal courtrooms (p. 410). However, in 1988, the Judicial Conference of the United States agreed to an experiment using video cameras to create official records in federal courts.[7] In addition, in 1989, cameras were allowed into military courts on an experimental basis.[8]

CONTROLLING PREJUDICIAL PUBLICITY

Access to Courtrooms

The Supreme Court and Access to Trials (pp. 420-424)

Several state appellate courts have recently affirmed the decisions of trial courts to open juvenile proceedings to the public (p. 423). In 1988 and 1989, the Supreme Courts of Arizona, Ohio, Vermont, and Virginia were among the courts to hold that the public could be present at juvenile proceedings. In Ohio, the Supreme Court said the statutory language, "the general public may be excluded" from juvenile proceedings, allows trial judges to decide that the public can be admitted. The Ohio Supreme Court said that a juvenile judge in Coshocton, Ohio, did not abuse his discretion when he decided to open a hearing to consider whether juveniles Daniel Fyffe and Bret McVay ought to be tried as adults. Fyffe and McVay, arrested for murder, argued that their Sixth Amendment rights to a fair trial would be jeopardized if evidence presented in an open hearing was ruled inadmissable during their trial. However, Juvenile Court Judge Fenning Pierce said the

---

[4]*E.g.*, Radio-Television News Directors Association, "News Media Coverage of Judicial Proceedings with Cameras and Microphones: A Survey of the States (March 1, 1989).

[5]"News Notes: State Activities," 16 Med. L. Rptr., June 13, 1989.

[6]"Court Reinstates Camera Experiment," 10 *News Media Update* 6 (July 8, 1989)

[7]"In Brief . . .," 14 *Access Reports* 14 (Oct. 19, 1988).

[8]"First Cameras in Military Courts," *News Media Update* 4 (April 15, 1989).

First Amendment right of the public to be in court includes juvenile trials. He said Fyffe
and McVay had not demonstrated that closing the hearing was necessary to protect their
Sixth Amendment rights.[9]

Juvenile proceedings are presumptively open to the public in 11 states, according to
the Reporters Committee for the Freedom of the Press. They are presumptively closed to
the public in about half of the states. Most of the others allow the judge to decide
whether the proceedings should be open or closed. In a few states, juvenile proceedings
are closed only in cases of the most serious charges. A few states allow the press, but not
the public, to attend juvenile proceedings.[10]

Access to Court Records (pp. 428-431)

The fight over the disclosure of sensitive court documents has intensified in recent
years.[11] The number of trials involving on such well-known persons as Oliver North,
Bess Myerson, and former New York Congressman Mario Biaggi is probably one reason.
Another may be that media companies can afford to be more aggressive because they are
spending less money fighting libel suits.

The large number of disputes over public access to pretrial and trial documents has
not substantially changed the law in the last few years. However, many courts are
holding that documents in both criminal and civil courts cannot be automatically sealed,
even when the information contained in them may not be offered in evidence at trial.

The U.S. Court of Appeals for the First Circuit said the federal rules governing civil
suits create a presumption that pretrial discovery should take place in public. Therefore,
in *Public Citizen v. Liggett Group*, the court said that documents surrendered in pretrial
discovery by the Liggett & Meyers Tobacco Company to the relatives of a lung cancer
victim could be made public. The First Circuit upheld the decision of a federal district
court to release to health associations 18 boxes of research documents prepared by a
consultant for Liggett & Meyers. The trial court had originally ordered that the
documents be made available to the relatives of the lung cancer victim who were suing
Liggett & Meyers but to no one else in order to protect the company's right to a fair trial.
However, the suit was dismissed before a trial could be held, and the documents were
never made public. Subsequently, a group of health organizations, including the
American Cancer Society and the American Heart Association, sued for access to the
research.

Liggett & Meyers claimed a general right of privacy in the documents and argued
that public access to pretrial discovery materials would excessively disrupt litigation.
The Public Citizen Litigation Group, representing the health organizations, said the
public should know as much as possible about the hazards of smoking.

---

[9]Ohio *ex rel.* Fyffe v. Pierce, 531 N.E.2d 673, 15 Med. L. Rptr. 2431 (1988); "Media Gain
Juvenile Court Access," *News Media and the Law* 21 (Spring 1989).

[10]"Media Gain Juvenile Court Access," *News Media and the Law* 21, 23 (Spring 1989).

[11]Lewin, "Press Curbs Increasing in Courts," *New York Times*, Feb. 8, 1989, at 1.

The First Circuit said federal rules permit the courts to seal pretrial documents in civil suits for "good cause" to protect persons "from annoyance, embarrassment, oppression or undue burden or expense." The court said the rules require that pretrial discovery be public unless compelling reasons justify denying public access.[12] The court noted that Liggett had not argued that documents sought by the health organizations contained trade secrets or other "specifically confidential material" that would have prevented them from being made public.

In contrast, two appellate courts have ruled that the news media have no right of access to search warrants and supporting documentation. In one of the cases, the U.S. Court of Appeals for the Ninth Circuit acknowledged that most documents related to a search warrant routinely become public after the warrant is served. However, the court said that neither the First Amendment nor the common law gives the news media even a qualified right of access to search warrants and related affidavits before an investigation results in an indictment. In *Times- Mirror Co. v. U.S.*, three news organizations sought access to search warrant records connected to Operation Ill-Wind, a nationwide FBI investigation into fraud and bribery in the procurement of military weapons. The Ninth Circuit, using First Amendment criteria from the Supreme Court's decision in *Press-Enterprise II* (p. 427), said that documents related to search warrants can be sealed because they have not traditionally been public. In addition, the court said, public access to documents related to search warrants would hinder criminal investigations in the same way that revealing other confidential information about investigations would.[13] Further, the court said, the common law provides no right of access when access is not traditional or when an important public need for access has not been demonstrated.

---

[12]Public Citizen v. Liggett Group, Inc., 858 F.2d 775, 789 (1988), *cert. denied*, 109 S.Ct. 838 (1989), *quoting* American Telephone & Telegraph v. Grady, 594 F.2d 594 (7th Cir. 1978).

[13]Times-Mirror Co. v. U.S., 873 F.2d 1210, 16 Med. L. Rptr. 1513 (1989), *modified*, "News Notes: Ninth Circuit Amends Search Warrant Access Ruling," 16 Med. L. Rptr. (Aug. 8, 1989). *See also*, Newspapers of New England Inc v. Clerk-Magistrate of Ware Div. of Dist. Court Dep't, 531 N.E.2d 1261 (Mass. 1988), *cert. denied*, 109 S.Ct. 2064 (1989). *But see, Re* Search Warrant for Secretarial Area Outside Office of Thomas Gunn, McDonnell Douglas Corp., 855 F.2d 569 (8th Cir. 1988).

10
PROTECTION OF NEWS SOURCES, NOTES, AND FILM

Courts in the last few years have usually employed the three-part test to determine whether to require testimony from reporters. The courts have said that persons seeking information from a reporter must demonstrate the relevance of the information sought to their case, a compelling need for the information, and the lack of an alternative source (pp. 442-450). In 1988, New York state's highest court ruled for the first time that journalists have a qualified privilege under both the state and federal constitutions to refuse to reveal nonconfidential information.

Maryland's shield law was substantially strengthened in 1988. In New Jersey and California, where courts have often narrowly interpreted state shield laws protecting journalists who choose not to testify, courts upheld the rights of reporters under the states' shield laws.

Journalists are weighing the significance of a Minnesota case that a source won after newspapers reneged on a promise not to publish his name.

In addition, police searched newsrooms in California and Minnesota in violation of state and federal laws.

PROTECTION UNDER THE CONSTITUTION: THE FIRST AMENDMENT

Application of the Three-Part Test

Civil Trials (pp. 447-450)

Early in 1988, New York state's highest court recognized a qualified privilege under both the state and federal constitutions for journalists refusing to provide information, even when they have not promised confidentiality to a source.[1] In *O'Neill v. Oakgrove Construction*, a civil case, the New York Court of Appeals said that a news photographer can refuse to provide unpublished pictures unless the person seeking the materials satisfied the three-part test developed by the courts since *Branzburg v. Hayes*. The New York court said the privilege is not destroyed because a photographer has not promised anyone confidentiality.

In *O'Neill*, the victim of an automobile accident, James O'Neill, sued the construction company working at the site of the mishap. O'Neill, seeking evidence to support his injury claim, obtained a court order requiring photographer Dennis Floss, of the Rochester *Democrat and Chronicle*, to provide the 58 pictures he had taken of the accident scene. The Court of Appeals recognized that the New York shield law did not protect Floss from a contempt-of-court citation for refusing to produce the photographs. The courts previously had interpreted the New York statute to provide protection only if a journalist promised confidentiality to a source (p. 456).[2]

However, the court of appeals said, "the ability of the press freely to collect and edit news, unhampered by repeated demands for its resource material," requires a qualified constitutional protection even if no promises of confidentiality have been made. The court ruled that O'Neill would have to prove the photographs he sought were highly relevant to his case, that they were critical to his claim, and that the information they provided was otherwise unavailable.

PROTECTION UNDER STATE STATUTES (pp. 452-459)

The Maryland state legislature amended that state's shield law in 1988 to allow journalists to withhold unpublished information and photographs and the names of sources who have not been promised confidentiality. The law expands protection beyond newspapers, journals, and the broadcast media to include wire services, news agencies, and "any printed, photographic, mechanical or electronic means of disseminating news

---

[1]O'Neill v. Oakgrove Construction Inc., 15 Med. L. Rptr. 1219 (N.Y. 1988).

[2]*E.g.*, Knight-Ridder Broadcasting Inc. v. Greenberg, 70 N.Y.2d 151, 518 N.Y.S.2d 595, 14 Med. L. Rptr. 1299 (1987) (New York Court of Appeals affirming cases cited on p. 456 of text).

and information to the public." The state incorporated into the new statute a three-part qualified privilege similar to that adopted by many courts.[3]

Court Interpretation (pp. 456-458)

In two states where the courts and the legislatures have fought over the protection to be given to journalists refusing to testify (p. 456), appellate courts have recently interpreted state shield laws favorably for journalists.

In New Jersey, the state's supreme court ruled that journalists are not required to testify about information already published. The court said *New Jersey Herald* reporter Evan Schuman did not have to appear in court to affirm a story about Gary Mayron's murder confession. The court said that the "plain language" in the state's shield law providing reporters with a privilege to refuse to disclose information "whether or not it is disseminated" does not conflict with state rules governing courtroom testimony. The court said "the legislature has continuously acted to establish the strongest possible protection from compulsory testimony for the press," particularly when the testimony is sought by the state (pp. 456-457).[4]

In California, a state court of appeal ruled that both the California constitution and the state's shield law protected a reporter who refused to give photographs of an automobile accident to one of the litigants in a civil law suit. Volkswagen of America had sought the pictures after a traffic accident victim claimed the van he was driving was not crash-worthy. The appellate court said journalists in California cannot be cited for contempt of court if they refuse to testify in civil suits when they are not involved in the litigation (pp. 457).[5]

BREACHING CONFIDENTIALITY (New section to be inserted after the summary on p. 459)

In the New Jersey and California cases mentioned above, the right of journalists to keep information confidential was challenged. In contrast, in the summer of 1988, a source who was promised confidentiality in Minnesota successfully sued two newspapers for revealing his identity. The source, Dan Cohen, won $700,000 after editors of the *Minneapolis Star & Tribune* and the *St. Paul Pioneer Post Dispatch* decided not to honor their reporters' promises of confidentiality.[6] The case has caused many reporters and editors to reevaluate the practice of pledging confidentiality.

---

[3]Md. Ann. Code sec. 9-112 (1988 Cum. Supp.).

[4]*In re* Schuman, 552 A.2d 602, 16 Med. L. Rptr. 1092 (1989).

[5]New York Times Co. v. Santa Barbara Super. Ct., 248 Cal. Rptr. 426, 202 Ca. App.3d 503, 15 Med. L. Rptr. 1576 (1988).

[6]See Cohen v. Cowles Media Co., 15 Med. L. Rptr. 2388 (Minn. 4th J.D.C. 1989), *aff'd in part*, as reported in "Newspapers Are Liable in Breach of Assurances of Confidentiality," *New York Times*, Sept. 6, 1989, at 15 (a state appeals court upheld $200,000 of the jury award for the breach of

Cohen, a public relations consultant and spokesman for the Independent-Republican gubernatorial candidate in Minnesota in 1982, offered four reporters a confidential tip six days before the election. Cohen, after being promised that his identity would not be disclosed, supplied each reporter with documents showing that the Democratic-Farm-Labor Party candidate had once admitted to shoplifting $6 worth of merchandise. Two news organizations--the Associated Press and WCCO-TV--did not identify Cohen as the tipster. But the editors of the *Star & Tribune* and the *Pioneer Post Dispatch* decided to name Cohen as the source of the story in spite of the promises of their reporters. The editors said that readers needed to know that the shoplifting story came from the candidate's opponent. They said the story of one candidate's campaign "releasing eleventh hour information" was more important than a story about a 12-year-old shoplifting charge that had been vacated.

When the stories appeared, Cohen lost his job as a public relations executive with an advertising firm and sued the newspapers for breach of contract and misrepresentation. Cohen contended the reporters' agreement with him met the legal requirements for a valid contract: 1) a promise by one person to do something, 2) that is accepted by a second person, 3) in exchange for a service. Cohen said the reporters' promises not to disclose his identity in return for the information about the gubernatorial candidate, an agreement that he accepted, was a binding oral contract. Cohen said the editors broke the contract when they published his name. Cohen also argued that the "revocation" by the editors of the reporters' commitment constituted a legal misrepresentation by the newspapers.

The Minnesota newspapers asked for summary judgment, which would have precluded a trial. They said that the agreements of the reporters to keep Cohen's name anonymous did not meet the technical requirements of Minnesota law governing contracts and misrepresentation. The newspapers also argued that the First Amendment immunized them from liability for any violation of contractual commitments.

However, a Minnesota trial court, referring to the U.S. Supreme Court's opinion in *Branzburg v. Hayes* (pp. 438-442), said that the First Amendment does not protect news organizations from violations of the law. Instead, the court said, Cohen should be given an opportunity to show that the newspapers' use of his name against his will was a breach of contract under state law. The court said a jury also would have to decide whether the newspapers' management or their reporters misrepresented the intent of the papers to meet the promise of confidentiality.[7] At the end of a trial, a jury awarded Cohen $200,000 in actual damages and $500,000 in punitive damages from the two papers for misrepresentation and breach of an oral contract.

Media attorney Floyd Abrams told the Associated Press that, unless the unprecedented Minnesota decision is reversed, the door is open for an "enormous range" of sources to claim "they've been victimized by the press."

---

contract claim, but reversed the lower court on the claim of misrepresentation and $500,000 in punitive damages).

[7]Cohen v. Cowles Media Co., 14 Med. L. Rptr. 1460 (Minn. 4th J.D.C. 1987).

At least one New York public relations firm has advised nearly 3,000 clients not to serve as anonymous sources for journalists.[8]

SEARCH WARRANTS (pp. 462-465)

In spite of statutes severely restricting the use of search warrants for unannounced searches of news rooms (pp. 464-465), at least a half-dozen news organizations have been subjected to unannounced searches in the last few years. Several searches took place in California and Minnesota.

In the California incidents, either the judge issuing the warrant or the officials conducting the search admitted they had erred. In one, Santa Clara county officials paid the *Viet Nam Nhat Bao* newspaper and the *Tan Van Magazine* $25,000 in compensatory damages after a search for evidence of violation of state welfare laws. Authorities not only seized business records in the 1987 raid, but also editorial matter such as unpublished manuscripts, photographs, and letters to the editor. The publisher of both publications said she was forced to miss deadlines and cancel one issue of the magazine. Santa Clara county officials paid the out-of-court settlement after admitting they should not have taken material unrelated to the allegations of welfare abuse. After another California search, one in San Bernardino County in 1988, the superior court judge who issued the warrant authorizing a search of the Riverside bureau of KCBS-TV later said the warrant was prohibited by state law. The judge ordered the county sheriff to return seized tapes that showed the ransacking of an animal research laboratory.[9]

In one of three Minnesota searches, a federal district court in Minneapolis ruled that the FBI's 1986 seizure of cameras from newspaper and television personnel after a drug raid was an unconstitutional prior restraint. The FBI feared that an undercover agent would be identified from film shot by the news staffs of the *Minneapolis Star & Tribune* and WCCO-TV. After the seizure, officials returned the film to both news organizations only on the condition that officials be allowed to examine the film and pictures before they were broadcast or published.

---

[8]"Anonymous Sources Given Advice," New York Times News Service (August 8, 1988).

[9]"FBI, Police Invade Newsrooms," *News Media & Law* 4, 5 (Fall 1988). *Also see* "Cops Confiscate Student Video of Shoot-out," *News Media & Law* 12 (Spring 1989).

11
ACCESS TO INFORMATION

The U.S. Supreme Court, in the most important development concerning access in 1989, said that FBI rap sheets are exempt from disclosure under the Freedom of Information Act. In another opinion, the Court said that federal agencies may not refuse FOIA requests simply because records in their possession are publicly available elsewhere.

The Supreme Court also sent back to a lower court a requirement that federal employees with access to classified information to sign security agreements. The requirement was one of many efforts during the Reagan administration to limit the amount of information available to the public. In another action, the government successfully prosecuted Samuel Morison for delivering classified photographs to a British magazine.

Congress countered one administration effort by passing the Computer Secrets Act, thereby taking control of computerized information out of the hands of the intelligence and defense agencies. In addition, the Reagan administration was embarrassed when documents obtained through the Freedom of Information Act revealed that the FBI, during the Reagan presidency, investigated groups opposed to the administration's policy in Central America.

The courts blocked some, but not all, of the efforts by federal agencies to prevent public disclosure of information and to prohibit organizations requesting information from receiving fee waivers.

ACCESS AND THE CONSTITUTION (p. 468)

Since *The Law of Public Communication* was published, judges have struck down restrictions on exit polling in at least seven states. The U.S. Court of Appeals for the Ninth Circuit ruled unconstitutional a Washington state statute prohibiting polling of voters within 300 feet of a polling place on election day. Federal district courts have overturned similar laws restricting the access of journalists and pollsters to polling places in Georgia, Kentucky, Minnesota, Montana, and Wyoming.[1] State appeals courts have struck down statutes in South Carolina and Florida.

The numerous state statutes reflect the opposition of election officials to television network projection of winners in presidential elections before the polls close in all states. Officials in western states, especially, argue that projections based on "exit polls" of voters reduce voter turnout for state and local elections held the same day.

In the Washington State case, the Ninth Circuit affirmed a lower court ruling that the state law violated the First Amendment (p. 473). In *Daily Herald v. Munro,* three television networks, the *New York Times*, and the Everett (Washington) *Daily Herald* had asked the courts to stop the enforcement of the state's restriction on exit polling. The Ninth Circuit said that exit polling constituted speech protected under the First Amendment because it involved the discussion of governmental affairs and the gathering of news. The court said the regulation of exit polling must be limited since it involves the regulation of speech content, the discussion of voting. The regulation of exit polling must also be restricted, the court said, because polling places are traditionally considered to be public forums for the discussion of public issues. Therefore, the Ninth Circuit said, the Washington state law must be narrowly tailored to accomplish a compelling governmental interest. The court acknowledged that the state had an interest in maintaining peace and order at polling places but said the Washington statute prohibiting polling with 300 feet of a polling place was too broad. The statute prohibited all exit polling, and not simply disruptive exit polling. The court said the state could also have limited its regulation by, for example, reducing the area off limits to pollsters.

Further, the Ninth Circuit said in *Daily Herald*, any state intent to prevent network projections of election results is unconstitutional. Regulating the exit polls because network projections "might indirectly affect the voters' choice is impermissible," the court said. It added that "a general interest in insulating voters from outside influences" could not justify the regulation of protected speech.[2]

Meanwhile, legislation seen by many officials as a way to settle the election projection controversy was introduced in Congress in 1989. In 1988 a bill that would have established a uniform closing time for polls during presidential elections passed the House of Representatives but not the Senate.

---

[1]NBC v. Cleland, 697 F. Supp. 1204, 15 Med. L. Rptr. 2265 (N.D. Ga. 1988); CBS v. Growe, 15 Med. L. Rptr. 2275 (D. Minn. 1988); NBC v. Colburg, 699 F. Supp. 241, 16 Med. L. Rptr. 1267 (D. Mont. *1988*). *See also,* "Media Win Challenges to Exit Poll Restrictions," 13 *News Media & Law* 22-23 (Winter 1989).

[2]Daily Herald Co. v. Munro, 838 F.2d 380, 14 Med. L. Rptr. 2332 (9th Cir. 1988).

ACCESS TO RECORDS

Federal Freedom of Information Act

History and Purpose (p. 477)

One of the most notable recent disclosures under the FOIA revealed that during the early 1980s the FBI conducted extensive surveillance of individuals and groups opposed to President Reagan's policies in Latin America. Documents obtained by the Center for Constitutional Rights disclose that the bureau used undercover agents, informers, and surveillance of peace demonstrations to investigate groups, including the Committee in Solidarity with the People of El Salvador (CISPES). FBI Director William Sessions acknowledged that the CISPES investigation might not always have been "properly directed." Sessions announced that he would discipline six bureau supervisors involved in the investigation and that the bureau would be willing to expunge names in the FBI's CISPES files.[3]

Reach of the Act: Defining Record *(p. 480)*

In January 1988, President Ronald Reagan signed the Computer Security Act, giving the National Bureau of Standards responsibility for monitoring the federal government's computerized records. The act instructs the agency to develop standards to insure the security of federal computer systems. However, the act prohibits government agencies from withholding computerized records from the public if they would be available under the FOIA as paper documents.[4]

The Computer Security Act was passed to block Reagan administration efforts to put the National Security Council in charge of regulating access to the federal government's computerized records. In 1984, Reagan established a committee dominated by the National Security Agency and military officials to recommend the means for protecting sensitive computerized government databases, including government information stored at private businesses. In 1986, then National Security Adviser John Poindexter directed all government agencies to limit access to "sensitive unclassified data," a move to block "hostile" countries from endangering national security by gaining access to government computers. Critics charged, however, that the Reagan administration was giving the National Security Council and the Department of Defense immense new power to restrict public access to information. Congressman Jack Brooks, a Democrat from Texas and author of the Computer Security Act, said that, in effect, the Reagan policy gave the Defense Department and the intelligence community "'Big Brother' control over all

---

[3]*E.g.*,"Report Said to Urge Punishment in Surveillance," *New York Times*, June 14, 1988, at 16; "FBI Papers Show Wide Surveillance of Reagan Critics," *New York Times*, Jan. 28, 1988, at 1; "FBI Is Willing to Erase Names from Its Records," *New York Times*, Sept. 17, 1988, at 5.

[4]Computer Security Act of 1987, Pub. L. 100-235, 101 Stat. 1724 (1988).

computer systems in the country."[5]   When Frank Carlucci succeeded Poindexter as National Security Advisor, he rescinded Poindexter's directive.

Procedures for Requesting Information

Agency Responsibility to Provide Records (New section to be added after the first paragraph on p. 483) In 1989, the U.S. Supreme Court ruled that an agency cannot withhold files being sought under the FOIA simply because the information is publicly available elsewhere. The 8-1 vote, upholding a decision of the U.S. Court of Appeals for the D.C. Circuit, means that the Justice Department must provide copies of all federal trial court opinions involving taxes to Tax Analysts, a non-profit organization that publishes information about tax law.

The Justice Department receives almost all federal court opinions affecting tax law because the department represents the federal government in tax litigation. The department had been giving Tax Analysts a list of pertinent district court decisions. However, the agency argued, it should not have to provide the court opinions themselves because they were already available at the individual district courts and because the cost of searching department files for the opinions would amount to $75,000 a year.[6]

Tax Analysts wanted the information for *Tax Notes*, a weekly magazine sent to tax attorneys, accountants, and economists. The organization had asked the Justice Department for the court opinions because it frequently had trouble obtaining them quickly from the "ninety-odd, far flung" federal district courts.

The Supreme Court said the Freedom of Information Act required that the court opinions be made available to Tax Analysts. In an opinion written by Justice Marshall, the Supreme Court declared that the court opinions were *agency records* under the meaning of the FOIA because the Justice Department had first obtained them and now controls them (pp. 480-481). The Court rejected a Justice Department argument that documents must be created by an agency in order to be considered *agency records* under the act. The Court said that the issue of whether an agency controlled a record depended only on whether the agency possessed the record, and not whether the agency originally produced the record.

The Supreme Court said the Justice Department improperly withheld the district court opinions from Tax Analysts because the opinions did not fit any of the nine exemptions of the FOIA. The Court said that Congress had not provided an exemption under the FOIA for documents available elsewhere. "If Congress had wished to codify an exemption for all publicly available materials," the Court said,

> it knew perfectly well how to do so. It is not for us to add or
> detract from Congress' comprehensive scheme, which already,

---

[5]"House Passes Measure to Protect Computers" 45 *Cong. Q.* 1400 (June 27, 1987); "Poindexter Refuses to Testify on Computer Security Policy," 45 *Cong. Q.* 513 (March 21, 1987).

[6]Tax Analysts v. Dep't of Justice, 845 F.2d 1060 (D.C. Cir. 1988).

"balances, and protects all interests" implicated by Executive Branch disclosure.[7]

Response Deadlines (p. 483) The U.S. Court of Appeals for the District of Columbia held in January 1988 that the Air Force Logistics Command could not routinely delay responses to requests filed under the FOIA. Between 1985 and 1987, Logistics Command officers consistently denied requests for abstracts of bids for government contracts to Payne Enterprises Inc., a company that sells information to prospective contractors. Logistics Command officers argued that the release of the information might result in escalating prices when bidders learned they had no serious competition. The Secretary of the Air Force routinely ordered the Logistics Command to release the information because it did not fit one of the nine FOIA exemptions. However, the Command took so long to release the documents that they were out of date by the time Payne received them. A federal district court refused to stop the Logistics Command delays because it said that Payne eventually received the information requested. However, the Logistics Command began to grant Payne's requests in a timely manner when Payne appealed the delays to the D.C. Circuit. Nevertheless, the court of appeals said the Logistic Command persistently hurt Payne's business by abusing the FOIA. The appeals court ordered the federal district court in Washington to consider issuing an injunction, if necessary, to prohibit similar delays.[8]

Fees (p. 484) Many journalists and research institutions have reported difficulties obtaining fee waivers under the provisions of the 1986 Freedom of Information Reform Act. The FOIA, as amended in 1986, exempts educational and scientific institutions and "representatives of the news media" from charges for searches made in response to FOIA requests (p. 484). The 1986 amendments also exempt anyone using the FOIA for a noncommercial purpose from certain copying fees and the cost of reviewing information for possible deletions. In addition, the amendments mandate that all fees be reduced or waived if the disclosure of information obtained under the FOIA is "likely to contribute significantly" to the public understanding of government.[9]

The Reporters Committee for the Freedom of the Press has said that most federal agencies have adopted Justice Department fee waiver guidelines that have been criticized by sponsors of the 1986 FOIA amendments as contrary to the spirit of the legislation (p. 485).[10] The Reporters Committee has charged that one agency tactic used to dodge fee waivers is to narrowly define *news media* when considering search fee exemptions.

---

[7]Dep't of Justice v. Tax Analysts, 109 S. Ct. 2841 (1989).

[8]Payne Enterprises v. U.S., 837 F.2d 486 (D.C. Cir. 1988).

[9]*See*, A. Adler, ed., *Litigation under the Federal Freedom of Information Act and Privacy Act* 161 (13th ed. 1988).

[10]"Agencies Issue Final Fee Rules," *News Media & Law*, 31-33 (Fall 1987).

However, a federal appeals court said in 1989 that sponsors of the 1986 FOIA amendments intended the phrase "representative of the news media" to apply to any persons or organizations regularly providing information to the public. The U.S. Court of Appeals for the District of Columbia ruled that the search fee exemption for the *news media* is available to any FOIA user who "gathers information of potential interest" to the public, uses editorial skills to create a distinct work, and publishes or otherwise distributes the work.[11] The D.C. Circuit, in *National Security Archive v. Department of Defense*, applied the news media exemption to a nonprofit research institute that disseminates information about foreign, defense, and international economic policy. The court held that the National Security Archive must receive a fee waiver from the Defense Department. The court said the Archive obtains information from several sources, exercises editorial judgment, creates indices and other research tools, and makes its work available to the public. The D.C. Circuit said the Archive's intent to sell its work did not constitute commercial use that disqualifies the organization from the fee waiver. The court said the Archive's sale of its information is no different, under the FOIA, than the sale of a newspaper.

In an earlier case, a federal district court ruled that a foreign publication also qualifies as *news media* even if it does not disseminate information in the United States. The U.S. District Court for the District of Columbia directed the FBI to waive the search fees for the *Southam News*, a Canadian newspaper seeking documents that explained why Canadians were denied entry to the United States as subversives. District Court Judge Harold Greene also ordered the FBI to waive copying costs, dismissing as "absurd" the FBI's contention that the publication of records explaining U.S. immigration policies would not significantly contribute to the public's understanding of government.[12] Several months later, Judge Greene ordered the FBI to show why it should not be held in contempt when the records had not been given to the *Southam News*. Greene, however, accepted the agency's argument that its failure to comply with the court order was due to an oversight by a U.S. attorney.[13]

In yet another instance, the CIA admitted that it mishandled a request to waive $600 in search fees made by Tim Peek, the managing editor of the Addison County, Vermont, *Independent*. Although Peek was investigating possible CIA ties to Middlebury College, the agency said the fee waiver request did not meet an agency requirement that the documents sought relate to current events. After a Senate hearing, the CIA admitted it misjudged the public interest in the Peek request and erred when it judged Peek to be a representative of a commercial publishing company.[14]

11Nat'l Security Archive v. Dep't of Defense, 1989 U.S. App. LEXIS 10945 (D.C. Cir.).

12Southam News v. Immigration and Naturalization Serv., 674 F. Supp. 881, 892 (D.C. D.C. 1987).

13"In Brief . . .," *Access Reports*, June 15, 1988, at 9. *See also*, "In Brief . . ., " *Access Reports*, May 31, 1989, at 8.

14Popkin, "Running the New 'Improved' FOIA Obstacle Course," 28 *Colum. Journalism Rev.* 45 (July/August 1989).

Exemptions

1. National Security (p. 487) In a case related to national security, but not the FOIA, a federal appeals court upheld the first conviction under federal espionage and theft statutes for the disclosure of classified information to the news media. Many journalists fear the case may impair their ability to obtain information from federal employees.

Samuel Loring Morison was convicted of selling classified photographs and summaries of intelligence reports to *Jane's Defense Weekly*, a prominent British defense magazine (p. 492). He was sentenced in U.S. District Court to two years in prison. Morison, a civilian employee at the Naval Intelligence Support Center at Suitland, Maryland, worked in a vault closed to anyone who did not have a "top secret" security clearance. In the summer of 1986, he took from a nearby desk in the vault satellite photographs of a Soviet aircraft carrier that were stamped "secret." Morison's fingerprints were found on the photographs, which had been given to *Jane's*. In addition, an analysis of his typewriter ribbon revealed that he had typed for *Jane's* a summary of a secret report about an explosion at a Soviet naval base . Investigators also found "secret" intelligence reports on the explosion in his apartment.

The government charged Morison with violating the 1917 Espionage Act by intentionally giving information pertinent to the national defense to "a person not entitled to receive it" and by refusing to give national defense documents to federal officials. The government also charged him with stealing and selling government photographs and records in violation of a federal theft statute. Morison had also violated a pledge not to disclose classified information, the government said.

The U. S. Court of Appeals for the Fourth Circuit said it could find no evidence in congressional documents or court opinions to substantiate Morison's contention that the Espionage Act applies only to "classic spying" and not to leaking documents to the press. In addition, the Fourth Circuit rejected Morison's contention that the prohibition in the 1917 Espionage Act against disclosing "national defense" information violates the First Amendment because it is vague and overbroad (p. 49). The court said Morison could not claim that he did not know he was violating the statute because he was an experienced intelligence officer who had been taught the regulations protecting the security of national defense information. The court also said that the term "national defense" in the Espionage Act, as defined by the trial court, applied to no more materials than necessary to protect the government's interest in national security, and therefore was not unconstitutionally overbroad.

The Fourth Circuit also turned aside Morison's argument that his First Amendment rights would be violated if he was prosecuted under the federal theft statute for giving stolen documents to the press for public dissemination. Judge Donald Russell said the First Amendment does not protect someone who steals records in order to give them to the press rather than to an enemy government. If that was the case, the judge said, the First Amendment would be converted "into a warrant for thievery." The Fourth Circuit also rejected the argument that Morison did not violate the statute prohibiting theft because he took *information* rather than tangible *property*. The court said the photographs and records Morison stole were tangible property as well as information.[15]

Although Morison violated a secrecy oath and took government property, some observers believe that his conviction may frighten federal employees who want to talk about government wrongdoing, even if they do not violate an oath or take property. Critics of the *Morison* decision argue that government employees will refuse to release even unclassified national defense information for fear of prosecution under the espionage laws. *New York Times* columnist Anthony Lewis suggested, for example, that the logic used by the appeals court could mean that a Defense Department employee could have been prosecuted for espionage for revealing to the press a White House plan to sell arms to Iran in exchange for hostages.[16]

The Reagan administration not only prosecuted Morison, but it also worked harder than any previous administration to obtain security pledges from government employees (see pp. 491-492). In May 1988, Reagan's efforts to obtain promises from federal workers that they would not disclose classified information received the approval of Federal District Court Judge Oliver Gasch. A year later, however, the U.S. Supreme Court sent the case back to Gasch for further consideration because, it said, circumstances in the case had changed since the original ruling.

Judge Gasch's 1988 decision had derailed opposition from Congress and federal employee unions to the use of nondisclosure forms such as Standard Form 189. SF-189 exacted a promise that employees who had access to classified or "classifiable" information would not disclose it. Employees who violated the agreement could lose their security clearances or their jobs and be subject to criminal and civil sanctions.[17] A similar form, Form 4193, was being used by the Central Intelligence Agency.

Although SF-189 was first implemented in 1983,[18] it did not spark controversy until mid-1987. Then, the Reagan administration increased the pressure on the several employees who had not yet signed the form. Although nearly three-quarters of the eligible government employees had signed the nondisclosure form by September 1987, about two dozen had refused.[19] At least a few of the employees who refused to sign the

---

15U.S. v. Morison, 844 F.2d 1057, 15 Med. L. Rptr. 1369, *cert. denied*, 109 S. Ct. 259 (1988).

16"Silence by Law," *New York Times*, April 7, 1988, at 27.

17For example, see discussion of *Snepp v. United States* (p. 65).

18Presidential Directive on Safeguarding National Security Information, 9 Med. L. Rptr. 1759 (1983). Editor's note: SF-189 was implemented at the same time the Reagan administration tried to prohibit employees with particularly high-level security clearances from writing about their work without approval, even after they had left the government (p. 491). SF-189 was overlooked during the outcry that forced the administration to back away from the lifetime pre-publication review plan. *The Law of Public Communication* is inaccurate to the extent it suggests (p. 492) the administration used a pre-publication review contract in the early 1980s that it had initiated in 1981 for all government employees with access to classified information. Instead, in 1983, the administration began using the SF-189 nondisclosure form.

19See, *e.g.*, Fact Sheet on Standard Form 189, Classified Information Nondisclosure Agreement, U.S. Information Security Oversight Office (Oct. 15, 1987); "Suits Over Secrecy Oaths Prompt Reaganite Retreat," 11 *News Media & Law* 12-14 (Fall 1987).

form lost their jobs. Others lost their security clearances.[20] In August, one employee, A. Ernest Fitzgerald, obtained a court order delaying government punishment for his refusal to sign SF-189. Fitzgerald, an Air Force management systems deputy, first attained prominence in the late 1960s by revealing C-5A cost overruns. At about the same time Fitzgerald took his case to court, three government employee unions and several members of Congress sued to stop the use of both SF-189 and Form 4193. They contended the forms violated their constitutional rights to speak freely and to petition Congress. In December 1987, Congress cut off funds for implementing the forms.[21]

In May 1988, Judge Oliver Gasch said that Congress, by barring use of funds for SF-189, unconstitutionally interfered in the presidential power to conduct foreign policy. Gasch said that the President had the constitutional authority to protect national secrets as head of the executive branch and as Commander-in-Chief of the nation's armed forces. Gasch said congressional refusal to fund SF-189 intruded "dramatically" into the President's "sensitive and complicated" role in foreign policy and national security.[22]

However, before an appeal of Gasch's decision reached the Supreme Court, Judge Gasch declared the use of the undefined term *classifiable* in forms 189 and 4193 unconstitutionally vague.[23] At the same time he accepted a definition for *classifiable* that became a part of the nondisclosure forms.[24]

The Supreme Court, responding to the first Gasch decision in a *per curiam* opinion, said the judge must reconsider the challenges to the nondisclosure forms in the light of his second decision and related developments. But, the Court cautioned Judge Gasch not to decide whether congressional refusal to fund the nondisclosure forms unconstitutionally impaired presidential powers unless absolutely necessary. The Supreme Court said courts should be "extremely careful not to issue unnecessary constitutional rulings" in cases involving "the fundamental relationship" between the branches of the federal government.[25]

In a related matter, President Reagan said in early 1988 that American manufacturers of civilian satellites would be permitted to provide photographic equipment capable of taking detailed pictures of the earth. Until 1988, private companies in the United States had been barred from putting cameras into space satellites that could detect objects smaller than 10 meters wide. The Defense Department feared that detailed photographs would disclose military secrets. However, the Soviet Union markets satellite photographs that allow the identification of objects only about 5 meters wide. The French are planning to compete with the Soviets.

---

[20]*E.g., Air Force Times*, Sept. 14, 1987, at 3.

[21]Continuing Appropriations, Fiscal Year 1988, Pub. L. No. 100-202 [H.J.Res. 395], 1010 Stat. 1329 (1987).

[22]Nat'l Fed'n of Fed. Employees v. U.S, 688 F. Supp. 671 (D.C. D.C. 1988).

[23]Nat'l Fed'n of Fed. Employees v. Garfinkel, 695 F. Supp. 1196 (D.C. D.C. 1988).

[24]52 Fed. Reg. 48367 (1987).

[25]Am. Foreign Service Ass'n v. Garfinkel, 109 S. Ct. 1693 (1989).

The Reagan decision could provide improved photographs for journalists, scientists, geographers, agricultural specialists, and urban planners. Some journalists, however, doubt that the federal government would permit news organizations to use photographs taken with powerful satellite cameras. The executive branch is expected to clear proposals for the photographic equipment only on a case-by-case basis.[26]

6. Personnel or Medical Files (p. 499) In 1988, a federal appeals court ruled that the recorded voices of the astronauts aboard the doomed Challenger shuttle flight are not "personal information" that can be withheld by the government. A three-judge panel of the U.S. Court of Appeals for the D.C. Circuit held that NASA must release the tapes of the Challenger crew recorded just before the craft exploded on January 28, 1986. However, the panel's decision was appealed, and the case will be heard by all judges of the D.C. Circuit.[27]

In *New York Times v. NASA*, the paper said it sought access to the tapes to provide the public a better understanding of the space tragedy than is possible through the already public transcripts of the crew's words.[28] The *Times* argued that the public could decide whether the noises of the Challenger and the voice inflections of the astronauts verified NASA's conclusions that the sounds of the Challenger were not unusual and that the astronauts had no warning of the explosion to come.

In court, NASA admitted that the Challenger tapes did not contain information about the private lives of the astronauts or their families. However, NASA argued that the personal nature of each astronaut's voice was enough to qualify the tapes as "personnel, medical or similar" files under Exemption 6 of the FOIA. NASA argued the release of the tapes would invade the privacy of the astronauts' families through "an intrusion which certainly would exacerbate feelings of hurt and loss."

The panel of D.C. Circuit judges, however, ruled 2-1 that the sound of a human voice is not "personal information." The court's majority admitted that the U.S. Supreme Court had broadly interpreted "similar files" under Exemption 6 to mean any government-held information about an individual and not just highly personal, intimate information (see p. 499). However, the D.C. Circuit said that for a record to be withheld, it must contain information about a person. The court's majority said that to accept the argument that the human voice is "personal information" would be to hold that every tape recording of audible human utterances, regardless of its content, is invariably a similar file because every person's voice is unique.

7. Law Enforcement Investigations (p. 503) The U.S. Supreme Court, in 1989, said that FBI "rap sheets" on private individuals are exempt from disclosure under the Freedom of Information Act, even if the information exists in state or local public records. The FBI's rap sheets contain an individual's history of arrests, indictments,

---

[26]*E.g.*, Licensing of Private Remote Sensing Space Systems, 54 Fed. Reg. 1945 (1989) (reopening discussion of regulations at 15 C.F.R. Part 960); Brender, "High-Resolution Remote Sensing by the News Media," 11 *Technology in Society* 1-10 (1989); "Sharper Pictures Promised from Space," *Broadcasting*, Jan. 25, 1988, at 50.

[27]New York Times Co. v. NASA, 860 F.2d 1093 (D.C. Cir. 1988).

[28]852 F.2d 602, 15 Med. L. Rptr. 2012 (1988).

acquittals, and convictions, information that is a matter of public record in local and state law enforcement agencies and courthouses across the nation. However, the FBI's rap sheets are a nationwide computer compilation of individual criminal records that have been traditionally kept confidential (pp. 507-508).

The Supreme Court's decision in *Reporters Committee for Freedom of the Press v. Department of Justice* ended a decade-long search by the Reporters Committee and CBS correspondent Robert Schackne for the criminal records of Charles Medico and his three brothers. The family's company, Medico Industries, was known by the Pennsylvania Crime Commission as "a legitimate business dominated by organized crime figures." Schackne wanted to know the connection between the company's defense contracts and bribery allegations against former Rep. Daniel Flood, a Democrat from Pennsylvania.

The FBI released the rap sheet information on three of the Medico brothers after they died. However, the agency refused to release the records of the only living brother, Charles Medico. Schackne and the Reporters Committee argued that the information in the FBI rap sheets was a matter of public record in local government files, and therefore ought to be released. In contrast, the Justice Department said the release of individual criminal records would violate FOIA Exemption 7, which permits withholding information that "could reasonably be expected to constitute an unwarranted invasion of personal privacy" (pp. 503, 506-507). The Justice Department was upheld by a federal district court but reversed by the U.S. Court of Appeals for the District of Columbia.

The U.S. Supreme Court, balancing the importance of individual privacy against the public interest in understanding government operations, unanimously overturned the appeals court decision. The Court ruled that Medico's records could be withheld under the privacy exclusion of Exemption 7 even though the rap sheets contained information that had previously been disclosed to the public. The Court's opinion, backed by seven justices, said that any FOIA request for the law enforcement records of a private citizen could reasonably be expected to invade the individual's privacy. Going even further, the Court said any request for a person's criminal records that does not seek "official information" about a government agency is an *unwarranted* invasion of individual privacy under Exemption 7.[29]

Therefore, the Supreme Court ruled the privacy provision of FOIA Exemption 7 protects all individual rap sheets and not just Medico's. The Court asserted that "the privacy interest in maintaining the practical obscurity of rap-sheet information will always be high." It said a case-by-case examination of individual circumstances is not necessary.

The Supreme Court said that centralized criminal records are private even though the information in them is available individually elsewhere.[30] The Court's opinion, written by Justice Stevens, said that individuals can have an interest in limiting the wider

---

[29]Dep't of Justice v. Reporters Comm. for Freedom of the Press, 109 S. Ct. 1468, 16 Med. L. Rptr. 1545, 1551 (1989).

[30]Reporters Comm. for Freedom of the Press v. Dep't of Justice, 816 F.2d 730, 14 Med. L. Rptr. 1108 , *modified on rehearing*, 14 Med. L. Rptr. 1908 (1987).

dissemination of personal information that is already publicly available. Justice Stevens said that computers allow the accumulation and storage of information that "would otherwise have surely been forgotten." Stevens said that the information collected in a centralized computer data base threatens privacy more than "bits of information" scattered in several police departments. He said that

> plainly there is a vast difference between the public records that might be found after a diligent search of courthouse files, county archives, and local police stations throughout the country and a computerized summary located in a single clearinghouse of information.[31]

Stevens said that if the information in the rap sheets was as publicly available as Schackne and the Reporters Committee contended, they could have easily acquired it without using the FOIA.

Stevens said other federal statutes and regulations have long recognized that computerized accumulations of information could endanger citizens' interest in privacy. He said the Privacy Act was passed "largely out of concern over 'the impact of computer data banks on individual privacy.'"[32] In addition, Stevens suggested, Congress has authorized the use of rap sheet information only in very limited situations, such as by law enforcement agencies, banks, and the nuclear-power industry. Stevens said the FBI's regulations specify that it can stop sharing rap sheet information with any agency that discloses the data to others.

Stevens also noted that both Congress and the Supreme Court have barred the release of information identifying citizens by name. The FOIA allows officials to delete details that would identify individuals in records otherwise disclosable. The Supreme Court's decision in *Department of Air Force v. Rose* (p.500) stressed the importance of safeguarding against the disclosure of information identifying individual cadets although it upheld the release of case summaries of honors and ethics code violations.

The Court acknowledged that citizens have a right to be told "what their government is up to." Therefore, "official information that sheds light on an agency's performance" should be disclosed under the FOIA. However, the Court said, the right of citizens to know about their government is not enhanced by the disclosure of information about private citizens "that reveals little or nothing" about agency conduct. The court argued that the disclosure of Medico's criminal record "would tell us nothing directly" about Congressman Flood's behavior or the conduct of the Defense Department when it awarded contracts to Medico Industries. The Court continued that,

> although there is undoubtedly some public interest in anyone's criminal history, especially if [it] is in some way related to . . . a

---

[31]*Id.* at 1552.

[32]*Id.* at 1553, *quoting* H.R. Rep. No. 93-1416, p. 7 (1974).

public official or agency, the FOIA's central purpose is to ensure
that the *Government's* activities be opened to the sharp eye of
public scrutiny, not that information about *private citizens* that
happens to be in the warehouse of the Government be so
disclosed.[33]

The Court said the Medico story did not serve the kind of public interest intended by
Congress when it enacted the FOIA.

Justice Blackmun concurred in the judgment in *Reporters Committee* but said that
the wording of the FOIA and its legislature history, as well as subsequent case law, did
not support the exemption of all rap-sheet information from disclosure. In an opinion
joined by Justice Brennan, Blackmun suggested that the Court's opinion would, for
example, prohibit the disclosure of a rap sheet revealing a congressional candidate's
conviction of tax fraud. Blackmun said candidates relinquish the right to keep such
information from the public when they choose to run for election. Blackmun said his
alternative to the majority's "categorical" exemption would be to "leave the door open for
the disclosure of rap-sheet information in some circumstances.

Journalists reacted sharply to the Court's decision. Veteran Supreme Court reporter
Lyle Denniston said the ruling "could shut off press access to a vast amount of
newsworthy information in federal government files."   Denniston said it was
"astonishing" to be told by the Supreme Court that information about individuals who
have had contact with the government "is not the kind" of information the FOIA was
designed to provide. Denniston said that

in the eyes of virtually any editor or reporter, the fact that a
member of Congress has ties to or does favors for someone who
has been in trouble with the police, or the fact that the Pentagon
buys goods or services from such a person, says a great deal
indeed about the member of Congress or about the Pentagon.[34]

In addition, Denniston questioned whether the disclosure of accumulated data would
interfere with personal privacy any more than the disclosure of scattered pieces of
information. In the past, press representatives have contended that the biggest threat to
individuals from computerized files is not disclosure by the press, but misuse by the
government. Journalists argue that public oversight of government records is the best
way to protect against abuse.[35]

---

[33]*Id.* at 1556.

[34]"The Press & the Law: Court Bans FOIA Probe of Central Files," *Wash. Journalism Rev.*
10 (May 1989).

[35]*E.g.*, Kirtley, "Is Big Brother Coming?," 3 *Statewide (California) Bench/Bar/Media
Newsletter* 6 (June 1988).

12
ELECTRONIC MEDIA

The law affecting the electronic media has changed substantially in the last two years and more change is expected soon. The deregulatory mood of the Federal Communications Commission may be waning with the arrival of a Bush-appointed commission. In addition, Congress appears ready to re-regulate portions of both broadcasting and cable television.

Congress, the executive branch, and the courts continue to battle each other on at least four fronts--the fairness doctrine, broadcast indecency, children's advertising, and dial-a-porn.

In addition, in August 1989, Congress was considering efforts to limit violence on television and amend the 1984 Cable Communications Policy Act.

The FCC recently adopted new procedures for choosing a broadcast licensee from competing applicants. The Commission also has broadened the spot news exemption of the equal opportunities rule for political candidates. In addition, the commission has decided to allow broadcasters to purchase exclusive rights to television programs to help protect them from the competition of cable.

Meanwhile, a federal appeals court has declared that governments may impose local programming requirements on cable companies.

82

REGULATION OF BROADCASTING

The Federal Communications Commission (pp. 531-541)

President Bush has appointed three Republicans to the Federal Communications Commission. Bush named Alfred C. Sikes, former head of the National Telecommunications and Information Administration, to be the chair of the commission. He also appointed Sherrie P. Marshall, a Washington attorney, and Andrew C. Barrett, an Illinois Commerce Commission member. All three have been confirmed by Congress.[1]

In the fall of 1989, one Democratic position on the commission remained to be filled. The term of Patricia Diaz Dennis expired in June 1989. The term of the other Democrat on the commission, James H. Quello, expires in 1991.

Enforcing Policy

Renewal Challenges (pp. 538-541) In March 1989, the FCC took the first step toward changing the highly criticized comparative renewal process, the commission's procedure for determining whether a broadcast license will be renewed or given to a competing applicant. The commission adopted rules to reduce the chances that challengers can obtain money from license holders willing to bargain in order to avoid lengthy and expensive comparative renewal proceedings.

Under the new rules, the FCC will only approve negotiated settlements between a licensee and a competing applicant if payment to a challenger willing to withdraw is limited to "legitimate and prudent" expenses. In addition, the FCC said it would only approve payments when settlements are made after the completion of a comparative hearing. The FCC said the two limitations on settlements should significantly reduce the number of competing applications filed in order to make quick profits through negotiations with a broadcast licensee. In addition, the commission is asking for more information about a challenger's financial qualifications and ownership plans in order to determine whether a competing applicant is a legitimate candidate for a license.[2]

In late 1989, the commission was also considering a revision of the rules governing what broadcasters must do to receive credit for "meritorious" service during comparative hearings (p. 539). In addition, the commission was evaluating a highly controversial proposal to use a lottery to decide between competing broadcast applicants.

---

[1]*E.g.*, "FCC Gains a Deregulatory Diplomat," *Broadcasting*, Aug. 14, 1989, at 29.

[2]Formulation of Policies and Rules Relating to Broadcast Renewal Applicants, Competing Applicants, and Other Participants to the Comparative Renewal Process and to the Prevention of Abuses of the Renewal Process, BC Docket No. 8-742 (May 16, 1989) (Westlaw, FCOM-FCC).

Regulation of Political Candidate Programming

Equal Opportunities for Political Candidates

"Use" of Broadcast Time (p. 545) The U.S. Court of Appeals for the D.C. Circuit in 1987 affirmed the FCC's policy that an appearance on a news show by a journalist who is running for office constitutes a "use" of a broadcast station by a political candidate.

In *Branch v. FCC*, the D.C. Circuit said that news about political candidates, not a candidate's reporting of the news, is exempt from the equal opportunity requirements of Section 315.[3] The court affirmed the FCC's ruling that appearances by reporter William Branch required Sacramento television station KOVR to provide equal time to Branch's opponents. Branch, who appeared on the air about three minutes a day, wanted to keep his job while he ran for a town council position in Loomis, California. KVOR said that it was unwilling to provide the 33 hours of airtime it would take to meet the equal opportunities requirements of Branch's opponents during the election campaign. The station said Branch would have to take an unpaid leave of absence during his political campaign.

Exempt Programming: Newscasts, News Interviews, and Documentaries (p. 547) The FCC has ruled that "Entertainment Tonight" and "Entertainment This Week" are *bona fide* news programs exempt from the equal opportunities rule. Both shows provide spot news coverage and news interviews about the entertainment world. The commission said the news exemption to Section 315 is not based "on the subject matter reported" in a show but on "whether the program reports news of some area of current events." The commission said that any effort on its part to determine "whether particular kinds of news are more or less bona fide would involve an unwarranted intrusiveness into program content and would be, thus, at least suspect under the First Amendment."[4]

Exempt Programming: Spot Coverage of News Events (p. 549) In 1988 and 1989 the FCC extended the spot news exemption for political coverage to two more forms of debates. The FCC said that coverage of debates sponsored by political parties and political candidates can be exempt from the equal opportunities requirement as well as debates sponsored by third parties. The commission said that the factor determining whether a debate is exempt under section 315 is its *bona fide* news value and not its sponsor. The commission's decisions mean debates no longer must be sponsored by a broadcast station or an independent party such as the League of Women Voters.

In 1989, the commission ruled that debates between presidential candidates George Bush and Michael Dukakis were exempt from the equal opportunities requirement even though they were sponsored by the two major political parties. The commission rejected a complaint by minor party presidential candidate Lenora Fulani. The FCC said debates

---

[3]824 F.2d 37 (D.C. Cir. 1987), *cert. denied*, 108 S. Ct. 1220 (1988).

[4]Request for Declaratory Ruling by Paramount Pictures Corp., 3 FCC Rcd 245 (1988).

can be exempt as long as broadcasters make good faith journalistic decisions that the debates are newsworthy. Televised debates, the commission said, do not give the candidates "unbridled power" to advance their candidacies. "Indeed, the adversarial nature of the debate format reduces greatly the chance of any broadcast favoritism."[5] In 1988, the commission exempted the televising of a debate sponsored by Dukakis and Richard Gephardt, two candidates for the Democratic party presidential nomination.[6]

In 1987, the U.S. Court of Appeals for the D.C. Circuit said minor-party candidates for president and vice president do not have a right to participate in televised debates. The court affirmed the FCC's decision to reject the complaint of the 1984 nominee for the Citizens Party, Sonia Johnson, who was excluded from the presidential debates between the Republican and Democratic candidates sponsored by the League of Women Voters. Johnson finished fifth in the election with less than 1 percent of the vote.

The D.C. Circuit said the FCC had not gone beyond its statutory authority in determining that debates between qualified political candidates are news events exempt from the equal opportunity requirements (pp. 549-550). The court, relying heavily on the U.S. Supreme Court opinion in *CBS v. Democratic National Committee* (p. 565-566), said that no individual has a First Amendment right of access to the broadcast media. The court said that the reasonable access (pp. 552-555) and equal opportunities requirements in the communications act "ensure that political debate will not be monopolized by one or a very few candidates." The act ensures "that all candidates from all points of the political spectrum will be able to utilize the media."[7]

Regulation of Public Issues Programming: The Fairness Doctrine (pp. 555-574)

The fairness doctrine, although declared dead by the FCC in 1987, is far from buried. In 1989, both the Senate Commerce Committee and the House Energy and Commerce Committee approved bills that would make the fairness doctrine statutory law. In July, the House Committee attached the bill as a rider to a major budget bill.[8]

A few months earlier, however, the U.S. Court of Appeals for the District of Columbia, in *Syracuse Peace Council v. FCC*, upheld the commission's 1987 decision to abolish the fairness doctrine. Until the FCC's decision in *Syracuse Peace Council*, the fairness doctrine had mandated that broadcasters must 1) provide programming on controversial issues of public importance and 2) insure that a diversity of views is presented (p. 556).

---

[5]*In re* Fulani, 65 P & F Rad. Reg.2d 644, 645 (1988), *quoting* Henry Geller, 95 FCC 2d 1236, 54 Rad. Reg.2d 1246 (1983), *aff'd sub nom.* League of Women Voters v. FCC, 731 F.2d 995 (1983).

[6]Request for a Declaratory Ruling by WCVB-TV, 63 P & F Rad. Reg.2d 665 (1987).

[7]Sonia Johnson v. FCC, 829 F.2d 157 (1987).

[8]*E.g.*, "Congress Returns to Full Fifth Estate Plate," *Broadcasting*, Aug. 14, 1989, at 32.

Eliminating the Fairness Doctrine (new section to be substituted for The Fairness Doctrine in 1987 on pp. 573-574)

Syracuse Peace Council The U.S. Court of Appeals for the D.C. Circuit said in *Syracuse Peace Council* that the FCC could eliminate the fairness doctrine because the commission adequately demonstrated that the policy did not serve the public interest.[9]

A divided three-judge panel said the FCC's decision to eliminate the fairness doctrine in *Syracuse Peace Council* was not arbitrary and capricious. The court said that, given the ambiguity of the issues, the FCC could rely on its assessment of the "net effect" of the fairness doctrine. The court accepted the commission's conclusions that the fairness doctrine substantially deterred the discussion of public issues and that government should not interfere in broadcast programming judgments. The court also accepted the FCC's premise that the benefits of the fairness doctrine could be dismissed as "governmentally-coerced speech."

The majority of the D.C. Circuit panel refused to consider whether the fairness doctrine was unconstitutional. Relying on the legal principal that courts should decide cases on constitutional grounds only when necessary, two of the three judges said the commission's determination that the fairness doctrine was contrary to the public interest was a sufficient and independent reason for eliminating it. However, Judge Kenneth Starr said the commission's decision was necessarily tied to First Amendment considerations. Starr said that throughout the FCC's opinion the commission wrestled with the U.S. Supreme Court's constitutional interpretation of broadcast regulation in *Red Lion Broadcasting v. FCC* (pp. 526-529).

The *Syracuse Peace Council* case began as the only fairness doctrine dispute to be decided against a broadcaster in the 1980s. The FCC had ruled in 1984 that WTVH(TV) of Syracuse, New York, had broadcast advertisements promoting the construction of a nuclear power plant without providing an opportunity for opposing views (p. 560). However, in 1985, the commission issued a comprehensive report declaring the fairness doctrine to be unconstitutional and contrary to the public interest (p. 573). In 1987, the D. C. Circuit said the commission was arbitrary and capricious for insisting that the Syracuse television station disobeyed a policy the commission believed to be a violation of the First Amendment (p. 574).[10] The court said the FCC could avoid the constitutional question by declaring the Fairness Doctrine did not serve the public interest.

In the commission's second consideration of *Syracuse Peace Council*, in 1987, the FCC said the fairness doctrine would no longer be enforced because it conflicted with both the public interest and the First Amendment. The commission refused to separate

---

[9]Syracuse Peace Council v. FCC, 867 F.2d 654, 10 Med. L. Rptr. 1225 (D.C. Cir. 1989).

[10]Meredith Corp. v. FCC, 809 F.2d 863, 13 Med. L. Rptr. 1994 (1987). The D.C. Circuit said the same day that it would consider a challenge to the FCC's 1985 Fairness Report (p. 574). That challenge was vacated after the FCC ruled the fairness doctrine unconstitutional. See Radio-Television News Directors Ass'n v. FCC, 831 F. 2d 1148 (1987).

its discussion of policy and constitutional issues in *Peace Council*, arguing that they were "inextricably intertwined."

In *Peace Council*, the FCC said the fairness doctrine thwarted, rather than enhanced, the discussion of controversial public issues. The FCC said broadcasters feared that the commission would receive complaints that their controversial issues programming was not balanced. Broadcasters not only feared an FCC ruling in favor of a viewer or listener, but the expense and damage to reputation caused by a fairness inquiry initiated by the commission. In addition, the FCC suggested, the fairness doctrine "may have penalized or impeded the expression of unorthodox or unpopular opinions."[11] The commission said that several of the broadcasters who had been the focus of fairness doctrine inquiries aired particularly provocative opinions.

The commission also found that the fairness doctrine imposed substantial burdens on the editorial process of broadcast licensees. Quoting its 1985 Fairness Report, the commission

> repudiated the notion that it was proper for a government agency to intervene actively in the marketplace of ideas. The Commission found that the enforcement of the Doctrine requires the "minute and subjective scrutiny of program content," which perilously treads upon the editorial prerogatives of broadcast journalists. The Commission further found that in administering the Doctrine it is forced to undertake the dangerous task of evaluating particular viewpoints.[12]

The commission argued that the FCC's intrusion into the editorial judgments of broadcasters was not necessary to ensure the airing of diverse views on important public issues. The commission cited findings in its 1985 Fairness Report that "revealed an explosive growth" in the number and variety of information outlets since 1969.

The FCC also argued that the broadcast media ought to have the same constitutional protection as the print media (pp. 526-531). It said the application of the First Amendment should not focus on the difference between the printed page and the broadcast spectrum, but on the similar ways the media are used. In addition, the commission said the Supreme Court's 1969 decision in *Red Lion Broadcasting Co. v. FCC* departed from traditional First Amendment reasoning. The commission said the *Red Lion* assertion that rights of listeners were superior to rights of broadcasters violated a fundamental First Amendment tenet--that governmental intervention in the marketplace of ideas should not be tolerated. The commission said,

---

[11]Syracuse Peace Council, 63 P & F Rad. Reg.2d 541, 566 (1987).

[12]*Id.* at 569, *quoting* 1985 Fairness Report, 102 FCC 2d 145, 191.

The First Amendment was adopted to protect the people *not from the journalists, but from government.* It gives people the right to receive ideas that are unfettered by governmental interference.[13]

In *Peace Council,* the FCC not only eliminated the fairness doctrine requirement that stations provide contrasting views on controversial public issues, but it also abolished the so-called "first half" of the fairness doctrine, the requirement that broadcasters cover controversial issues of public importance in the first place (p. 570). The FCC said the two portions of the fairness doctrine were too interrelated to be separated. In addition, the commission said, the "first half" of the fairness doctrine duplicated another commission policy, the requirement that licensees cover issues important to their communities. Hence, there was no need to retain the "first half," the commission said.[14]

The elimination of the fairness doctrine in *Peace Council* also meant the abandonment of a subsidiary policy called the Cullman doctrine. The Cullman doctrine required that broadcasters provide contrasting views if only one side of a controversial issue was presented in sponsored programming--even if the licensee could not find a sponsor for a second viewpoint (pp. 562-563). *Peace Council* was, in fact, a Cullman doctrine case. WTVH originally had failed to provide free time for views at odds with an advertisement promoting the construction of a nuclear power plant.

The FCC's *Peace Council* decision left intact the personal attack and political editorializing rules (pp. 566-569).[15] The FCC suggested it was keeping fairness policies applied to elections, including the Zapple doctrine. The Zapple rule requires that the supporters of opposing political candidates be given approximately the same amount of airtime (pp. 569-570).[16]

The FCC's Confrontation with Congress The FCC's *Peace Council* decision may have satisfied a federal appeals court, but it did not satisfy Congress. Although the FCC contends that the fairness doctrine is a commission-initiated policy (p. 556) that the commission can drop, many members of Congress believe that only Congress can repeal the fairness doctrine. Several members of Congress believe that the fairness doctrine was incorporated into the 1934 Communications Act in a 1959 amendment.

The 1959 amendment to section 315 of the communications act exempted news programs from the requirement that broadcasters provide equal opportunities for political candidates. Congress qualified the exemption by adding that it should not be construed to relieve broadcasters, during news programming,

---

[13]*Id.* at 589 (emphasis in the original).

[14]*Id.* at 561-562 (1987).

[15]*See id.* at 555-556 n. 75 (1987). *See also* Syracuse Peace Council, 64 P & F Rad Reg.2d 1073, 1075 (1988) (The commission, on reconsideration, rejected a petition that it should declare at that time that the personal attack and political editorializing rules violated the First Amendment. The commission said it is considering in another proceeding whether the rules should be dropped).

[16]Syracuse Peace Council, 63 P & F Rad. Reg.2d at 555-556 n. 75).

from the obligation imposed on them under this Act to operate in
the public interest and to afford reasonable opportunity for the
presentation of conflicting views on issues of public importance.[17]

Although the 1959 amendment did not specifically refer to the fairness doctrine, the
FCC argued for the next twenty years that Congress added the fairness doctrine to the
statute through the amendment to section 315. The U.S. Supreme Court seemed to agree
when it upheld the constitutionality of the fairness doctrine in its 1969 *Red Lion* opinion.
In *Red Lion*, the Court said Congress "made it very plain" in the 1959 amendment that a
broadcaster's requirement to operate in the "public interest" imposed a duty "to discuss
both sides of controversial public issues."[18]

However, the FCC, in a deregulatory mood during the Reagan administration,
argued in the 1980s that the 1959 amendment did not codify the fairness doctrine. In
both the Report to Congress and the *Syracuse Peace Council* decision, the commission
pointed to a 1986 decision of the U.S. Court of Appeals for the D.C. Circuit,
Telecommunications Research and Action Center (TRAC) v. FCC.[19] The D.C. Circuit, in
TRAC, said that the congressional adoption of section 315 in 1959 only "ratified the
Commission's longstanding position that the public interest standard *authorizes* the
fairness doctrine."[20] The court said the 1959 amendment demonstrates that Congress
considered the fairness doctrine to be an obligation created by the FCC, and "not as a
fixed requirement frozen in place by the Act." The 1959 amendment did not, according
to the D.C. Circuit, mean that the duty to be fair had become part of the 1934
Communications Act, as the Supreme Court had implied in *Red Lion*. Because the
fairness doctrine was created by the commission, the commission has the authority to
eliminate it, the D. C. Circuit said. The Supreme Court denied *certiorari* in *TRAC*, a case
that involved far more than the interpretation of the 1959 amendment. The Supreme
Court's denial of *certiorari* left the appeals court explanation of the 1959 amendment
intact.

If congressional intent in 1959 was in dispute, Congress has left no doubts about its
intent in the last few years. Congress responded to the FCC's 1985 Fairness Report by
prohibiting the commission from changing or eliminating the fairness doctrine before the
FCC reported fairness doctrine alternatives to Congress (pp. 573-574). However, the
FCC eliminated the fairness doctrine on the same day it issued the report required by

---

[17]47 U.S.C. sec. 315(a) (1982).

[18]Red Lion Broadcasting Co. v. FCC, 395 U.S. 367, 380-81, 1 Med. L. Rptr. 2053, 2059
(1969).

[19]Syracuse Peace Council, 63 P & F Rad. Reg.2d at 548 n. 46 and Fairness Report to
Congress, 63 P & F Rad. Reg.2d at 496 n. 32. *See* Telecommunications Research & Action Center
v. FCC, 801 F.2d 501, 13 Med. L. Rptr. 1881 (Cir. DC 1986).

[20]801 F.2d at 517-518, 13 Med. L. Rptr. at 1894 (emphasis added).

Congress.[21]   The commission eliminated the fairness doctrine knowing that Congress would object because just two months earlier Congress had passed a bill explicitly inserting the fairness doctrine into the 1934 Communications Act. That legislation had been vetoed by President Reagan (p. 573). After the FCC eliminated the fairness doctrine, Congress attached a rider to the continuing budget resolution of 1987 that would have again incorporated the policy into the communications act. However, Congress withdrew the rider when Reagan said he would not sign the bill with the fairness doctrine language included.

In 1989, key legislators were committed to insuring that the fairness doctrine was required by statute. However, President Bush has said that he, like Reagan, was prepared to veto legislation codifying of the fairness doctrine.[22]

Other Programming Regulation

Obscenity, Indecency, and Profanity (pp. 575-580)

Congress banned broadcast indecency in September 1988. However, early in 1989, the U.S. Court of Appeals for the District of Columbia Circuit enjoined the government from enforcing the ban until the court could consider arguments that the new law was unconstitutional.[23]

Congress, despite warnings that a law banning indecency would violate the First Amendment, ordered the FCC to prohibit indecent programming 24 hours a day.[24] The FCC said the new law left the commission "no discretion."[25] Before the new law, the commission had prohibited indecency only when there was a reasonable risk that children might be in the audience (p. 577).

Doubts about the constitutionality of the total ban on broadcast indecency were reinforced by a 1989 U.S. Supreme Court decision prohibiting a ban of indecent telephone messages. In *Sable Communications v. FCC*, discussed later in the chapter, the Supreme Court said that indecent communication could be regulated to protect children but could not be banned from adults.

Even before *Sable Communications*, the U.S. Court of Appeals in the District of Columbia had questioned the constitutionality of an FCC restriction on indecency that fell short of a ban. The FCC had proposed to permit broadcast indecency between midnight and 6 a.m., two hours less than before. However, in *Action for Children's*

---

[21]See Inquiry into Section 73.1910 of the Commission's Rules and Regulations Concerning Alternatives to the General Fairness Doctrine Obligations of Broadcast Licensees (hereinafter referred to as Fairness Report to Congress), 63 P & F Rad. Reg. 2d 488 (1987).

[22]"Bush seen as sending signal on fairness doctrine," *Broadcasting*, April 17, 1989, at 31.

[23]"Chances slim for 24-hour FCC ban on indecency," *Broadcasting*, Jan. 30, 1989, at 58.

[24]Making Appropriations for the Departments of Commerce, Justice, and State, the Judiciary, and Related Agencies for the Fiscal Year Ending September 30, 1988, Pub.L. No. 100-459, sec. 608, 102 Stat. 2216, 2228 (1988)

[25]Enforcement of Prohibitions against Broadcast Obscenity and Indecency in 18 U.S.C. sec. 1464, FCC 88-416, Westlaw FCOM-FCC (1988).

Television v. FCC, the D.C. Circuit said that the commission had not proven that children would be listening to the radio or watching television before midnight.[26]

Until April 1987, the commission had not punished indecency broadcast after 10 p.m. because it assumed that few children would be in the audience (p. 580). However, the FCC said in April 1987 that broadcasters could not assume that broadcasting indecency after 10 p.m. would be "safe."[27] A few months later, the commission said broadcasters could safely air indecent programming only after midnight.[28]

In *Action for Children's Television*, the D.C. Circuit said the FCC had not adequately explained why broadcasters could only air indecency between midnight and 6 a.m. The court vacated warnings the commission had issued to two radio stations for broadcasting indecent programming about 10 p.m. The court noted that while the FCC had previously based its indecency decisions on the need to protect children 12 years old and younger, the commission was justifying its new policy on the viewing habits of young people 12 and older. If the commission had decided to protect children older than 12, the court said, it needed to explain why. In addition, the D.C. Circuit said, the FCC needed to provide data on the number of children in the audience of the radio stations considered in violation of the indecency policy rather than data for all radio stations in the markets.

The FCC abandoned its plans to respond directly to the D.C. Circuit's decision after Congress banned indecency 24 hours a day.[29] But, after the court's opinion, the commission decided not to fine a Kansas City, Missouri, television station for broadcasting an "indecent" movie at 8 p.m. The commission said it had been instructed by the D.C. Circuit to withhold action against evening programming until it could document the listening and viewing habits of children.[30] In June 1988, the commission had said that the broadcast of the movie, "Private Lessons," was indecent because it contained "explicit" nudity in a pandering and titillating manner.

The D.C. Circuit, although it did not accept the FCC's midnight to 6 a.m. "safe harbor" for broadcast indecency, did uphold the commission's decision to expand its enforcement of indecency to more than the repetition of "seven dirty words." Until the spring of 1987, the commission had limited its enforcement of indecency to the repetitive use of sexual or excretory expletives such as "shit" and "fuck." However, in April 1987, the FCC said that "patently offensive" programming other than the repetitive use of dirty words would be subject to penalties.

---

[26]852 F.2d 1332 (1988).

[27]*E.g., In re* Regents of California, 2 FCC Rcd 2703, 2704, 62 P & F Rad. Reg.2d 1199, 1201-1202 (1987).

[28]Infinity Broadcasting Corp. of Pennsylvania, 3 FCC Rcd 930, 931 n.47, 64 P & F Rad. Reg.2d 211, 219 n.47 (1987).

[29]Enforcement of Prohibitions against Broadcast Obscenity and Indecency in 18 U.S.C. sec. 1464, FCC 88-416, Westlaw FCOM-FCC (1988).

[30]FCC, "KZKC (TV), Kansas City, Mo, Apparently Liable for $2,000 for Indecent Broadcast," July 23, 1988 (news release); "FCC Drops Fine for Indecency in KZKC Case," *Broadcasting*, Aug. 14, 1989, at 59-60.

In April 1987, the FCC said that KCSB-FM of Santa Barbara, California, had illegally broadcast indecency when it aired the song, "Making Bacon," by the Pork Dukes. The song contained explicit sexual language, including invitations to oral and anal sex. At the same time FCC warned KPFK(FM) of Los Angeles that its broadcast of excerpts from the play, *The Jerker*, were indecent. The play featured detailed descriptions of homosexual fantasies. The FCC also warned that WYSP(FM) of Philadelphia had broadcast indecency during the morning show of "raunch radio" personality Howard Stern (p. 580). The FCC said Stern used such expressions as "limp dick" in a "pandering and titillating fashion." The FCC only warned the stations, rather than imposing penalties such as fines, because it said broadcasters may have been led to believe that the commission would tolerate the programming.[31]

For more than a decade, the FCC had defined *indecency* to be the description or depiction of sexual or excretory activities or organs in ways patently offensive to "contemporary community standards for the broadcast medium." In *Action for Children's Television*, the D.C. Circuit affirmed the FCC's decision that its past policy to permit offensive programming not containing the seven dirty words made "no legal or policy sense." The court rejected the argument that the FCC's definition of *indecency* was unconstitutionally vague. The court said the commission's definition was substantially the same one found constitutional by the U.S. Supreme Court in *FCC v. Pacifica Foundation* in 1978. The D.C. Circuit also rejected an argument that the FCC's indecency regulation was unconstitutionally overbroad because it could apply to programs of "serious merit." The court said that programs of "significant social value" could still contain offensive language and descriptions, and therefore could be channeled to times when children might not be listening. Indecent programming, whether it has "serious merit" or not, the commission said, qualifies for First Amendment protection and therefore must be channeled rather than banned.

In August 1989, the FCC initiated indecency actions against "shock jock" programs on three radio stations. The commission asked radio stations KSJO(FM) of San Jose, California, WFBQ(FM) of Indianapolis, and WLUP(AM) of Chicago to reply to an FCC letter telling them that they may have violated the federal indecency statute. All of the programming used double entendres to address explicit sexual subjects. The FCC could fine each station up to $2,000.[32]

The FCC, since 1987, has said that several sexually-related references in programming during children's viewing hours did not meet the commission's indecency criteria. The commission refused to take action against radio station WTMA of Charleston, South Carolina, for broadcasting the world "clocksucker" in a political advertisement opposing the purchase of a clock for city hall. The commission said the ad

---

[31]*In re* Pacifica Foundation, Inc., 2 FCC Rcd 2698, 62 P & F Rad. Reg.2d 1195 (1987); *In re* Regents of California, 2 FCC Rcd 2703, 62 P & F Rad. Reg.2d 1199 (1987); Infinity Broadcasting Corp. of Pennsylvania, 2 FCC Rcd 2705, 62 P & F Rad. Reg.2d 1202 (1987).

[32]"FCC Turns Up the Heat on Indecency, *Broadcasting*, Aug. 28, 1989, at 27.

did not involve a "patently offensive depiction of sexual or excretory activities or organs."

The commission also dismissed a complaint against WTRG-FM in Rocky Mount, North Carolina, for broadcasting the song, "I Want to Kiss Her, But . . . ." The commission said that innuendo and double entendres are punishable only if they are intermingled with explicit sexual references that allow only a sexual interpretation. The FCC also ruled that a television broadcast about high school sex education in Seattle was not patently offensive even though it included frank discussions of sexual topics, the use of sex organ models, and the simulated demonstration of birth control devices. The FCC said the program, broadcast by KING-TV, was not indecent because the references to sexual and excretory organs and activities were not "vulgar," "lewd," or "shocking." Nor did the sexual references pander or titillate, the commission said.[33]

Children's Programming (pp. 582-583)

In the late summer of 1989, both houses of Congress were considering proposals aimed at regulating children's programming on television. Most would limit the amount of advertising aired during children's programming and impose on broadcasters a requirement to provide children's programming.

In 1988, Congress passed a bill regulating children's television only to have it pocket-vetoed by President Reagan in November. The 1988 bill would have limited the amount of advertising time during children's programming to 10 1/2 minutes per hour on weekends and 12 minutes on weekdays. It also would have required broadcasters to serve "the educational and informational needs of children." Although the bill was supported by broadcasters, President Reagan said it was "counterproductive" and violated the First Amendment.[34]

A year before, in October 1987, the FCC initiated a rule-making proceeding into children's advertising that has not been completed. The commission, responding to issues raised in two rulings by the U.S. Court of Appeals for the D.C. Circuit and petitions from Action for Children's Television, said it would examine commercial time limits for children's programming and the so-called program-length commercials.[35] The first ruling of the D.C. Circuit, in June 1987, ordered the FCC to justify a 1984 decision to abolish time limits on commercials during children's programming (pp. 582-583). The limits, similar to the proposed 1988 legislation, had restricted advertising during children's programming to 9 1/2 minutes per hour on weekends and 12 minutes on weekdays.

In the second related D.C. Circuit opinion, in October 1987, the court overturned an FCC decision protecting "program-length commercials," saying that the commission had

---

[33]"FCC Rejects Five Indecency Complaints," *Broadcasting*, April 11, 1988, at 37.

[34]"Reagan Vetoes Bill Putting Limits on TV Programming for Children," *New York Times*, Nov. 7, 1988, at 1.

[35]Revision of Programming and Commercialization Policies, Ascertainment Requirements, and Program Log Requirements for Commercial Television Stations, 2 FCC Rcd 6822 (1987).

betrayed the congressional intent of the 1934 Communications Act (p. 581). Section 317 of the statute, known as the sponsorship identification requirement, provides that broadcasters must identify anyone who provides money, services, or something else of value toward a program. The FCC had ruled that a station did not have to announce that the manufacturer of "He-Man and Masters of the Universe" had provided the station a children's cartoon with the same name.

In *National Association for Better Broadcasting v. FCC*, a Los Angeles-based citizens group claimed that KCOP-TV did not tell viewers that "He-Man" was, in effect, sponsored programming. "He-Man" is based on fantasy characters created and produced by Mattel and Group W Productions. The companies provide the show to KCOP in exchange for two minutes of advertising time during the station's children's programming. The practice of trading a program for advertising spots, known as bartering, was responsible for 70 percent of children's syndicated programming in 1983.[36]

In *NABB v. FCC*, the National Association for Better Broadcasting argued Mattel and Group W provided a "great benefit" to KCOP-TV when it offered the station a popular program in exchange for only two minutes of advertising. The producers of the program spent $14 million on the first 65 episodes of "He-Man," but the total advertising time was worth about $400,000.

The FCC, relying on its 1974 children's program policy statement (p.582), said the barter arrangement did not violate section 317 of the communications act. The commission, quoting the 1974 statement, said the arrangement with KCOP-TV would have violated the sponsorship identification rule only if the show "He-Man" was so closely connected to "He-Man" advertising "that the entire program constitutes a single commercial promotion." The commission said that "He-Man" contained "significant entertainment value for child audiences." The agency said it "could see 'no useful purpose in restricting unnecessarily presentations of programs merely because products are depicted therein.'"[37]

However, the D.C. Circuit said the commission could not avoid requirements to disclose sponsors by hiding behind the 1974 children's programming policy. The sponsorship identification rule applies to all programs, the court said. The court added that, given the prevalence of barter arrangements for children's programming, the FCC must devise a standard to determine when a barter agreement does not constitute program sponsorship. The court said that the commission must have a guideline to determine when interests of the broadcaster and the program producer are so balanced in an exchange that the arrangement is "immunized" from the sponsorship-identification rule.

36Nat'l Ass'n for Better Broadcasting v. FCC, 830 F. 2d 270 (1987).

37*Id.*, *quoting* Action for Children's Television, 58 P & F Rad. Reg.2d 61, 67 (1985).

Miscellaneous (pp. 585-586)

In the late summer of 1989 both houses of Congress passed bills designed to reduce depictions of violence on television. The bills would exempt from antitrust action meetings of representatives of the broadcast, cable, and film industries so that they could establish standards for program content. The Senate approved a bill aimed at sex and drug abuse on television as well as violence. The House of Representatives approved a bill targeting violence only.[38]

In May 1988, the FCC warned broadcasters to adhere to the provisions of the 1934 Communications Act banning payola. The commission was responding to a letter from a House Telecommunications Subcommittee member, Jack Fields, of Texas, who expressed concerns about the "reemergence of payola."

The communications act prohibits anyone from offering or accepting money to air programming without the knowledge of a station manager or owner. The statute requires stations to disclose any payments they receive to broadcast specific programming. Violators can be jailed and fined up to $10,000.[39]

CABLE

The Cable Communications Policy Act of 1984 (pp. 594-595)

In 1989, a federal appeals court declared for the first time that the regulation of cable programming is constitutionally permissible. In the meantime, pressure was mounting in Congress to re-regulate cable television.

The Design (pp. 595-596)

Since the U.S. Supreme Court's 1987 decision in *City of Los Angeles v. Preferred Communications, Inc.* (pp. 595-596), lower courts have disagreed about the constitutionality of regulations authorized in the 1984 Cable Act. However, in July 1989, the U.S. Court of Appeals for the Seventh Circuit became the first federal appeals court to approve local government regulation of cable programming.

The Seventh Circuit upheld a fine of $60,750 levied against three affiliated cable television companies that failed to provide locally originated progamming as required by their franchise with the city of Chicago. The three companies, known jointly as Chicago Cable TV or CCTV, were granted franchises in three of the five cable service areas in Chicago. They were required to provide 4 1/2 hours a week of cable programming produced in Chicago specifically for Chicago audiences. However, CCTV instead provided programming produced by suburban affiliates that "would be interesting to" Chicago customers, found to be unacceptable by the Chicago Cable Commission.

---

[38]*E.g.,* "Congress Returns to Full Fifth Estate Plate," *Broadcasting,* Aug. 14, 1989, at 31.

[39]"FCC Lays Down Law on Payola," *Broadcasting,* May 23, 1988, at 53.

In *Chicago Cable Communications v. Chicago Cable Commission*, CCTV argued that the city's local program origination requirements constituted impermissible content regulation under the First Amendment. However, the Seventh Circuit, relying on a Supreme Court decision in *United States v. O'Brien*, said Chicago demonstrated that the local programming requirement met a substantial government interest and that the requirement was no greater than necessary to serve that interest.

The Seventh Circuit said that, although First Amendment interests were "plainly" at stake, cable television can be regulated more than the print media. One reason, the court said, is that cable television systems must use the public streets and rights of way. In addition, the court suggested, the expense of cable facilities creates economic constraints that limit competition much as the physical constraints of the electromagnetic spectrum limit the number of broadcasters. The Seventh Circuit said that cable,

> like other forms of the electronic media, is an economically scarce medium. Unlike the traditional forms of print media, a cable programmer enjoys a virtual monopoly over its area, without the threat of an alternative producer.[40]

Therefore, the court continued, local governments, representing cable customers, are "duty-bound" to ensure that the few cable operators use their franchise optimally.

The Seventh Circuit accepted arguments by the city of Chicago that the local cable programming requirement met substantial government interests because it improved communications between Chicago citizens and their government and provided jobs for Chicago citizens, particularly minorities. The court said that the Chicago requirements will increase the number of outlets for community self-expression, an important government interest.

The court said that Chicago's local programming requirements are "really no greater" than necessary to further the governmental interests of increased local communications and increased employment. The court said the "city is not seeking a dominant interest" in cable programming "but simply a few hours a week." In addition, the cable companies are not required to provide "any specific program, kind of show, or editorial viewpoint." As long as the programs are geared to Chicago, the court said, the cable companies have "full discretion" over what they provide. The court said the cable operators retain "the ultimate decision" over which programs to air during the four and a half hours of local programming required.

In contrast to the Seventh Circuit's opinion, no federal appeals court has said that cable programming regulation is a violation of the First Amendment. However, at least

---

[40]Chicago Cable Communications v. Chicago Cable Comm'n, 1989 U.S. App. LEXIS 10766 (1989).

two California federal district courts have questioned the constitutionality of requirements that cable companies provide community access channels.[41]

Meanwhile, organizations including the National League of Cities, the Consumer Federation of America, and the National Association of Broadcasters have asked Congress to increase regulation of cable television. The organizations claim that cable television is a monopoly that has abused its power. Bills would restore city authority to regulate cable rates, permit telephone companies to compete with cable, and require cable programmers to offer their products to companies using such technologies as microwave to disseminate programming into homes.

Programming Regulation

Access (p. 597) The community access channel has been restored in Kansas City, Missouri, after a dispute involving the Ku Klux Klan. The Klan had accused the city of violating the First Amendment and the 1984 Cable Act by preventing it from using the access channel. The Klan contended the city and the local cable company, in order to exclude Klan programming, illegally eliminated the access channel and substituted a channel with programming controlled by the cable operator. City officials and the cable company agreed to restore the access channel after a Missouri federal district judge refused to dismiss the Klan's complaint.[42]

Other Cable Programming Regulation (pp. 600-602)

The FCC has tried to use cable programming regulation to protect over-the-air broadcasting from an increasingly powerful cable industry. But the FCC's efforts have been blocked, in part, by the U.S. Court of Appeals for the D.C. Circuit.

In 1985 and 1987 the D.C. Circuit held unconstitutional FCC rules requiring cable system owners to carry the signals of local broadcasters. The FCC said that "must-carry" rules are needed to ensure that local broadcasters can be seen in their communities, especially when most viewers subscribe to a cable system. Without must-carry, the commission argued, cable operators might drop local broadcast stations and therefore severely weaken local broadcast service.

In both D.C. opinions, the court said the must-carry rules violated the First Amendment because the FCC had not sufficiently justified the need to protect local broadcasters from cable companies (p. 601). In addition, the court said, the rules were too broad, protecting local broadcasters more than necessary to insure local broadcast service.

[41]Group W Cable, Inc. v. Santa Cruz, 669 F. Supp. 954, 14 Med. L. Rptr. 1769 (N.D. Cal. 1987); Pacific West Cable Company v. Sacramento, 672 F. Supp. 1322 (E.D. Cal. 1987). *Also relevant*, Century Federal, Inc. v. Palo Alto, 684 F. Supp. 1465 (N.D. Cal. 1968), *appeal dismissed*, 108 S. Ct. 1002 (1988).

[42]Missouri Knights of the Ku Klux Klan v. Kansas City, 1989 U.S. Dist. LEXIS 7029 (1989); "K.C. Access Channel Restored After Klan's First Amendment Victory," Cable TV and New Media, August 1989, at 3.

However, the court's 1985 opinion, *Quincy Cable TV, Inc. v. FCC*, said that some must-carry rules might be constitutional. Therefore, in 1987, the FCC redrafted must-carry rules to make them less burdensome for small cable operators and included a sunset provision that would automatically terminate the rules after 5 years (pp. 601-602). In addition, the FCC required cable operators, for the first time, to provide subscribers with switches that would allow viewers to shift easily from watching television via cable to watching over-the-air broadcast signals. Under the rules, cable operators had to educate subscribers about the use of what are called A/B switches and offer to help install them. The commission argued that once viewers were familiar with the A/B switch, they would have easy access to local, over-the-air broadcast signals even if the stations were not carried on the cable system.

In 1987, in *Century Communications v. FCC*, the D.C. Circuit acknowledged that the FCC had significantly changed the must-carry rules after *Quincy* However, the court said the FCC still had not undertaken the necessary fact-finding to determine whether cable operators would drop local stations if there were no must-carry regulations. In addition, the commission assumed, rather than proved, the court said, that television viewers subscribing to cable believe they can only watch over-the-air television signals through their cable system. The court said the commission argued without evidence that cable subscribers need five years to learn that they can get off-the-air signals easily through the use of an A/B switch.[43]

A few months later, the D.C. Circuit ruled that, although it had struck down the 1987 must-carry rules, its holding did not affect the A\B switch and consumer education requirements.[44] Soon afterwards, the FCC rewrote the A/B switch and education rules so that they could stand on their own as of November 1989.[45]

Although cable companies are now free from must-carry rules, the FCC has adopted another regulation limiting cable programming options. As of January 1990, if not delayed by an appeal, broadcasters can purchase exclusive rights to syndicated television programs, an option already available to cable operators and superstations such as WTBS(TV) of Atlanta and WGN-TV of Chicago. The commission's ruling, issued in May 1988, allows a local television station to buy rights to popular programs such as "Magnum P.I." or "M.A.S.H." and block the local cable system from carrying the program on other channels. According to the rules, a cable system must substitute a different program for any syndicated show purchased by a broadcaster with exclusive rights. Before the new rule, the re-runs of many popular syndicated programs were often available on several channels at different times of the day in many markets.

---

[43]Century Communications Corp. v. FCC, 835 F.2d 292, 14 Med. L. Rptr. 2049 (D.C. Cir. 1987), cert. denied sub nom. Office of Communication of the United Church of Christ v. FCC, 108 S.Ct. 2015 (1988).

[44]Century Communications Corp. v. FCC, 837 F.2d 517 (D.C. Cir. 1988).

[45]Amendment of Part 76 of Commission's Rules Concerning Carriage of Television Broadcast Signals by Cable Television Systems; Amendment of Part 15 of the Commission's Rules Concerning Input Selector Switches Used in Conjunction with Cable Service, 4 FCC Rcd 4552, 66 P & F Rad. Reg.2d 790 (1989).

As part of the same action, the FCC expanded the protection from competition available to the network programming of local broadcasters (p. 600). Even before 1990, the FCC had required cable operators to protect local broadcast stations from the competition of network programs aired on stations from outside of the local viewing area. The commission had said that cable systems must substitute other programming for a network program, such as "LA Law," that can be seen on a "distant signal" at the same time the program is broadcast by local stations. Now, in addition, the commission rules require cable operators to substitute for a network program available on a "distant signal" that duplicates a program offered by local affiliates at any time. Cable systems with fewer than 1,000 subscribers, about half of the total, will be exempt from the new rules.[46]

The commission, by adopting the program exclusivity rules for broadcasters, reinstated a policy eliminated in 1980. At that time, the commission did not consider the cable industry a threat to traditional broadcasting. However, since 1980, the number of persons watching traditional television programming from local stations and the networks has decreased as viewers for other cable services have increased. Cable advertising revenues have soared during the same time. The commission said the new rules encourage a larger variety of programming on cable and give local over-the-air broadcasters the chance to compete equally with networks and cable operators.

In addition, in 1989, the commission asked Congress to repeal the compulsory copyright license for cable use of both local and distant broadcast signals. The commission recommended the elimination of a government-established price for the right of cable operators to retransmit broadcast signals. Instead, cable operators would negotiate the price of individual programming with programmers and broadcasters.[47]

COMMON CARRIER REGULATION

Telephone (pp. 604-605)

The U.S. Supreme Court said in 1989 that a federal statute banning the use of interstate telephone lines for indecent dial-a-porn violated the First Amendment. The Court said Congress could constitutionally ban dial-a-porn that is legally obscene.

The Supreme Court unanimously agreed with Sable Communications, which provides recorded dial-a-porn messages, that a congressional ban on indecent dial-a-porn was unconstitutional. Congress had tried, in 1988, to eliminate the business of providing both indecent and obscene explicit sexual messages to callers for a charge, for adults as well as minors. Congress said that the companies providing obscene messages could be

---

[46]Amendment of Parts 73 and 76 of the Commission's Rules Relating to Program Exclusivity in the Cable and Broadcast Industries, Report and Order, 3 FCC Rcd 5299, 64 P & F Rad. Reg.2d 1818 (1988), *clarified*, Memorandum Opinion and Order, 66 P & F Rad. Reg.2d (1989).

[47]Bruce, "FCC Watch," *Cable TV and New Media*, July 1989, at 2.

fined up to $500,000 and spend up to two years in jail. The providers of indecent messages could be fined as much as $50,000 and jailed up to six months.[48]

In *Sable Communications v. FCC*, the Supreme Court acknowledged that Congress has a legitimate interest in preventing children from being exposed to dial-a-porn. But, said Justice Byron White, who wrote the Court's opinion, indecent speech is constitutionally protected and therefore any regulation of dial-a-porn must be strictly limited. Congress invalidly banned all dial-a-porn instead of only restricting access by children, the court said. White said it was "another case of burning the house to roast the pig."[49]

The Court rejected arguments that nothing less than a total ban could prevent children from listening to indecent dial-a-porn. The Court pointed out that the FCC had devised a combination of restrictions on dial-a-porn in 1987 designed to limit access by minors while allowing access by adults. The FCC had said that dial-a-porn companies would have to restrict access by children by requiring callers to use either a credit card or an access code, or by scrambling calls so that they could be heard only through a descrambling device (pp. 604-605). The U.S. Court of Appeals for the Second Circuit agreed in 1988 that the commission's rules were a "feasible and effective" way to protect children from dial-a-porn.[50]

The Supreme Court's majority in *Sable* said the FCC's rules had not been adequately tested because of the congressional dial-a-porn ban. The Court rejected the argument that it should defer to Congress, which had implied--by passing the dial-a-porn ban--that the FCC's rules would not sufficiently protect children from telephone indecency. The majority said the Court must protect the First Amendment against a statute that restricted speech more broadly than necessary.

The Court also rejected the argument that the Court's own opinion in *FCC v. Pacifica Foundation* provided a precedent for a ban of indecent dial-a-porn. The Court's *Sable* opinion said that *Pacifica* only allowed indecent programming to be regulated, not banned. In addition, the Court said in *Sable* that *Pacifica* applied to over-the-air broadcasting, where persons turning on the radio or television could be "surprised" by an indecent message they might not have a "meaningful opportunity to avoid." In contrast, the Court said, dial-a-porn could not be imposed on a "captive audience." Dial-a-porn, the Court said, requires the listener to take "affirmative steps to receive the communication," including dialing the telephone number.

The Court in *Sable* upheld the congressional ban on obscene dial-a-porn by a 6-3 margin. White said the Court had repeatedly refused to consider obscene speech to be

---

[48]Child Protection and Obscenity Enforcement Act of 1988, 102 Stat. 4502, section 7524, enacted as Title VII, Subtitle N, Anti-Drug Abuse Act of 1998, Pub. L. 100-690 (Nov. 1988), *amending* Telephone Decency Act, Pub. L. 100-297, 102 Stat. 424 (April 1988).

[49]Sable Communications of California, Inc. v. FCC, 109 S. Ct. 2829 (1989). *Cf.* Mountain States Telephone and Telegraph Co., v. Arizona Corp. Comm'n, 773 P.2d 455 (Ariz. 1989) (state regulations blocking commercial information services with prior subscription violates freedom of expression under state constitution).

[50]Carlin Communications, Inc. v. FCC, 837 F.2d 546 (1988).

protected by the First Amendment. The Court rejected an argument made by Sable that Congress had created an unacceptable national standard of obscenity in the dial-a-porn legislation. The Court said the constitutional requirement of the U.S. Supreme Court in *Miller v. California* (pp. 373-74), that obscenity be based on community standards, applied to all federal statutes banning obscenity. If Sable's calls originate from different communities with different local standards, the Court said, Sable must insure that the messages available to any community are not considered to be obscene in that community. The Court said the Constitution permits legislation that requires a dial-a-porn service to ensure that each community receives calls that are not obscene by local community standards.

Justice William J. Brennan, Jr., dissenting from the obscenity ruling in *Sable*, argued that banning any dial-a-porn, whether it is indecent or obscene, is unconstitutional. Brennan, in an opinion joined by Justices Thurgood Marshall and John Paul Stevens, accepted the need to protect children from dial-a-porn. But the dissenters suggested the regulatory alternatives the FCC had devised could be used to limit the access of minors to both indecent and obscene dial-a-porn while allowing access for adults.

Even before the 1988 congressional ban on dial-a-porn, the FCC could prosecute dial-a-porn providers allowing persons under 18 years old to use their services (p. 604). In 1988, the FCC fined a dial-a-porn provider for the first time. Audio Enterprises, Inc., of San Jose, California, was not only fined $50,000, but also agreed to stop its service until it could effectively deny access by minors.[51] One woman complained to the FCC that six children, ranging from 10 to 13 years old, had spent 211 minutes listening to Audio's dial-a-porn service. Following the call, the woman's 10-year-old daughter was sexually molested by two brothers. The woman said her daughter had encouraged the boys with language the girl had heard during the call.[52]

The telephone companies themselves are also trying to restrict dial-a-porn providers. In January 1988, AT&T stopped payment to sponsors of commercial pornographic messages. Sponsors of those services had received from 2 to 5 cents a call from AT&T. Some phone companies, such as Illinois Bell, refuse to bill for dial-it services they consider objectionable. Others, like Pacific Bell, Mountain Bell, and New York Telephone Company, offer customers the option of blocking access to dial-it services from their telephones.[53] In April 1988, an Arizona telephone company's ban on sexually explicit message services was allowed to stand when the U.S. Supreme Court denied a petition for *certiorari* challenging the policy.[54]

---

[51]Audio Enterprises, Inc., 65 P & F Rad. Reg.2d 1035 (1988).

[52]Audio Enterprises, Inc., 64 P & F Rad. Reg.2d 1681 (1988). A similar proceeding initiated against a second dial-a-porn business had not been concluded by summer 1989. *See also* Intercambio, Inc., 64 P & F Radio Reg.2d 1663 (1988).

[53]*E.g.*,"'Dial-a-Porn' Industry: Lucrative and Besieged," *New York Times*, June 24, 1989, at 7, and "Moves Taken to Restrict Dial-a-Porn," *New York Times*, January 19, 1988, at 11. Pacific and Mountain Bell come from materials in your file up to date 8-89

[54]Carlin Communications v. Mountain States Telephone and Telegraph Co., 829 F.2d 1291 (9th Cir. 1987), *cert. denied*, 108 S. Ct. 1586 (1988).

THE HYBRIDS

Subscription Television (STV) (p. 607)

In June 1988, the U.S. Court of Appeals for the District of Columbia affirmed an FCC ruling that subscription television and direct broadcast satellites (DBS) are not *broadcast* technologies.

The FCC said the term *broadcasting* in the 1934 Communications Act refers to communication to a general audience rather than to specific points of reception. Subscription television uses over-the-air broadcast signals, but the commission said that STV operators are not broadcasters because they provide programming to subscribers in a private, contractual relationship and encrypt their programming to prevent its unauthorized use. STV is therefore no longer subject to broadcast regulations such as the equal opportunities rule for political candidates. Neither is DBS, which could provide direct satellite-to-home communications (p. 807-808).

The court of appeals accepted the FCC's explanation for abandoning the traditional means of determining regulation--by the nature of the program content a service delivers. Instead, the FCC is basing its regulation of STV and DBS on the technology used to distribute the content, the court said.[55]

Early in 1988, a different panel of judges on the same court rejected a similar regulatory approach for ITFS, Instructional Television Fixed Services. ITFS licensees, who traditionally offer instruction to students at selected receiving locations, have been allowed to expand into commercial broadcasting in recent years. The D.C. Circuit said that the FCC has not adequately explained its attempt to classify ITFS as a nonbroadcast technology.[56]

---

[55]Nat'l Ass'n of Better Broadcasting v. FCC, 849 F.2d 665 (1988).

[56]Telecommunications Research and Action Center v. FCC, 836 F.2d 1349 (1988).